KILLING

A Spiritual Discernment Guide for Law Enforcement

RAY K. VANN

-SERVI-

Servi Publishing, LLC
Lufkin, TX

Servi Publishing, LLC

ISBN: 0-9600657-0-9
ISBN-13: 978-0-9600657-0-7

Dear God, please guide us always into Your perfect will, that we may be steadfast instruments of Your peace. Please show us what You want us to do, and bless us with an unwavering courage to do it. Amen.

DEDICATION

This book is dedicated to the men and women in blue who serve our country and most especially to my brothers and sisters, sworn and civilian, serving in the Lufkin Police Department.

CONTENTS

ACKNOWLEDGMENTS

Nothing of real value and truth is possible without the help of God. To Him I give thanks and praise!

I would be lost without Fe, my best friend and wife of 25 years. I thank Fe for her support during this project as well as the many other projects in my life. I also thank our daughters, Mary, Nikki and Kiahley, for always encouraging me.

I offer a very special thanks to my father, Raymond K. Vann, Sr., for his guidance and suggestions regarding this writing, and to my step-mother, Sandy, for correcting many, many of my mistakes.

I thank Rev. Gavin Vaverek, JCL, for his honest critique and straightforward advice. I also thank my bishop, Most Rev. Joseph E. Strickland, JCL, for allowing me to write about this somewhat controversial topic.

I offer thanks to retired NYPD Commissioner Bernard B. Kerik for his willingness to review this book and for his comments. I also offer thanks to retired Dallas PD Assistant Chief Vincent Golbeck for his very helpful suggestions and kind comments regarding this book.

Finally, I thank Gerald Williamson, Director of Public Safety for the City of Lufkin, and David Thomas, Chief of Police of the Lufkin Police Department for their guidance and suggestions, as well as Lt. Jerry Smith for his acceptance of me in the first Clergy and Police Alliance academy. In fact, without their willingness to allow me to be a member of the Lufkin Police Department, this book would not have been written.

INTRODUCTION

Killing another human being is a real possibility for those in law enforcement. While most law enforcement officers enjoy lifelong careers with no incidents that result in killing, the reality is that many do and all must face this possibility daily. This book is written primarily with law enforcement officers in mind. However, most of what is written is also of significant importance for any citizen who is regularly armed with any type of deadly weapon for the purposes of self-defense and/or defense of others. The topic of this book is a spiritual discernment on killing. More specifically, it highlights the importance of being prepared and working through the spiritual aspects or belief system issues associated with the possibility of having to end the life of another human being. For those who have already been in the situation of having to use deadly force, the topic is the same, but you will be working through it from a different perspective. The main purpose of this writing is to assist law enforcement officers in spiritual discernment so that any spiritual issues, known and unknown, can be addressed prior to encountering an incident where deadly force is needed. In addition, this writing will assist law enforcement officers in developing a plan of action to be implemented immediately after an incident where deadly force is used.

Most books have only a paragraph or two about the author set aside in a separate section outside of the main body of the writing.

And this works for most books. However, I realize that the group this book is written for, law enforcement officers, need to know the source before it can have any true credibility. So I would like to offer a little about me and why I am compelled to write this book. If you know a little about me, then hopefully what I offer in this book will be a little more credible.

You live in a world that most people don't even know exists. Sure, they watch television and go to the movies, they watch the news at night and read the newspaper, and they may even, on rare occasion, find themselves experiencing this other-world. You, however, live it, breathe it, smell it, feel it, and bathe in it every day that you are on duty. And when you are off duty, its residue permeates the fabric of your off-duty attempt to feel normal. So if I pretend to know your world, you will call *BS* on me before you get past the next paragraph. Sure, I visit your world often, but I am only a spectator most of the time. This allows me to experience some of the same experiences, but I do not have the weight of responsibility at the level that you have. I understand this and yet I know that you and I can still connect. So who am I?

I am a husband, a father of three daughters, an ordained permanent deacon for the Catholic Diocese of Tyler, Texas, and a police chaplain for the Lufkin Police Department in Lufkin, Texas. I earned a Bachelor of Arts degree in Theology and a Master of Arts degree in Theology from Saint Joseph's College in Maine, and I've earned my *Basics* commendation bar from the International Conference of Police Chaplains. I make a living serving as a consultant to small cities and counties in rural Texas.

If you are not familiar with the Catholic Church, we deacons are a little different than the deacons you may be familiar with. Deacons in the Catholic Church are ordained clergy. In most dioceses, men aspiring to be deacons spend five or six years in formation and education before they are ordained. Once ordained, we are ordained for life. We serve at mass, we preach, we baptize, we preside at weddings and funerals, but most of all, we are called to serve in our communities in works of charity much like Stephen and Philip in the biblical writing, Acts *of the Apostles*.

Unlike priests, most permanent deacons do not earn their

living working for the church. Most of us have secular employment. Also unlike priests in most circumstances, we can be married when we are ordained, but if we are not married when we are ordained, then we are called to a celibate life. Praise God, I was married when I was ordained! And still am. But, if a Catholic deacon's wife dies before him, then that deacon is to embrace a life of celibacy. So I take really good care of my wife!

Just like the original seven deacons of the *New Testament*, we are called to serve those whose needs are being ignored. We are to carry the Gospel of Jesus Christ to all people, not only by our words but mostly through our actions. We are called to service above all else. For me, I serve in many ways, but the ministry that I am particularly called to, the one that I have a true passion for, is police chaplaincy.

I am not your stereotypical clergyman. I believe that every person is called to holiness, not just the ordained. I also realize that the ordained clergy are not extra holy, we are just like you, but we are entrusted with the responsibility of leading the flock, and we are in very deep danger if we mislead you. And many of us do! Many officers have, or will at some point during their career, arrest a preacher. This is because we are human beings and some of us have not worked out all of our issues prior to ordination.

If I fail you due to lack of concern, lack of sincerity, lack of preparation, lack of prayer, lack of listing to God, then my soul is in deep danger. Jesus, speaking in the synoptic Gospels of Matthew, Mark, and Luke, makes it very clear, "It would be better for him if a millstone were hung round his neck and he were cast into the sea, than that he should cause one of these little ones to sin" (Lk 17:2, RSV-CE). *Little ones* means those who turn to us preachers for guidance in their faith. It is with this message in mind that I offer this writing.

In addition, I understand the world's view of the hypocritical Christian. Many only experience the Christian who acts one way on Sunday morning and then totally different on Monday. Or the Christian who curses you for pulling him over for speeding when he is running late for Wednesday evening church. Or the Christian who smiles that fake Christian smile to her friends and then berates the waitress after church for serving her unsweet tea instead of sweet tea.

I smile often, but I will not offer a fake, *I'm a good Christian* smile. If I'm ticked off, you will probably know it, even if we're at the church on Sunday. I try not to get ticked off, or act like a jerk, but I am human just like you. What point is it to be a different person on Sunday? Why say *God bless you* as you're leaving my church on Sunday, and then *F-you* when you cut me off in traffic on Monday. I try not to say that, but I am not perfect; just trying to become better. Any person, especially a preacher, who claims to be perfect, well, watch him closely.

So I'm not your stereotypical preacher and I couldn't care less about political correctness. In fact, I realize that what I am writing here is somewhat controversial for some. It may be outright alarming for others. And for even others, it may be seen as scandal. But they are not my concern, you are.

In reading, praying, and discerning, I realized that I can in no way write this book without presenting a biased opinion. In fact, to do so would be dishonest and to leave out the material that follows would be incomplete. This is one of the reasons why this book is divided into two parts. My goal is not to have you agree with me, but rather to have you consider all aspects of this subject for yourself as I have. My goal is to help you better understand your own current conviction regarding this matter, or to realize that you don't really have a conviction if that's the case, or to realize that you need to change your conviction, or simply reconfirm the conviction you already hold. *Part I* hopefully helps you do that while reflecting on the material you find in *Part II*.

In all of the reading and praying and discerning that I've done, my conviction has been reconfirmed and solidified. In fact, it is so strong that I can in no way write this as a neutral guide. Even if I try my best and leave my own convictions out, the way that I present my findings would be influenced by these convictions. You can read more about my personal discernment on killing in *Chapter Seven*.

So, I need to offer a disclaimer of sorts. I need to share with you my convictions regarding this subject so that you will receive honest guidance. Nothing drives me crazier than to have an instructor or writer with a political agenda who hides that agenda under a pretense of intellectualism. I have two daughters in college and they occasionally get these professors who present their opinions and agendas as facts that must be accepted. I myself have had these types of professors and read books from these types of authors. If you were to ask them if they are liberal or conservative, they would be outraged, stating that they are unbiased presenters of facts. The fact is that many, if not most, college professors are liberal and push a liberal agenda. I don't think they should push an agenda of any kind, nor should I, but I do believe that they should be honest about who they are so the students will know from what perspective they are teaching the class.

So, here's my disclaimer. I am a Christian and I will refer to the name of Jesus whenever I can. But I am not trying to convert you with this writing. I am a Catholic and although I am not proselytizing in this book, what I write comes from a Catholic Christian perspective. This is not a deep theological writing so it should not be an issue whether you are Catholic or Protestant or anything else in the Christian world. I've learned that although we Christians may do things in different ways, our beliefs are more alike than not. Catholics and Protestants can both agree that Jesus is our Lord and Savior and it is through Him that we enter Heaven. What's more important than that? And even if you are not Christian or not a believer of any kind, I am not on a mission here to jam Jesus into your life.

I write this book for everyone in law enforcement and I truly believe that regardless of your faith, you can gain valuable tools in reading these words. However, much of *Part II* is geared more toward Christians mainly because of the passive message that many Christians tend to preach and teach. Those who follow the teachings of Judaism and Islam, as well as Buddhism, Hinduism, and others can benefit from this writing but may not have some of the issues that we Christians have. Since I am not a follower of or specifically educated in these faiths, I will not pretend to know about something I don't. Yet, I do offer some research findings that may be of interest. So while I present some information regarding other belief systems, I am sticking mostly with Christianity. I certainly do not want to water down the issue by trying to completely cover all faiths. When you try to alter your message for everyone's ears, then nobody truly hears you. That being stated, let me also state that this will not be a preaching session in book form. This is a law enforcement training manual, not Sunday morning church material.

I am quite conservative in my politics, but I do not let these politics influence my faith. Rather, my faith influences my political opinions. I am armed at all times, train on a regular basis, and I will do whatever I must, including killing, to stop someone who is physically harming or about to physically harm me or another human being. I realize that chaplains, especially in the military, are usually unarmed. I also realize that the Roman clerical collar and a Glock 27 don't go together in the eyes of popular opinion. But I have to ask myself, "What concerns me more? How I may look on the evening news after justly killing an aggressor or how I may feel if that aggressor killed another person when I was able to stop it from happening but didn't?" Obviously, my life and the life of others are much more important than my reputation as portrayed by an agenda-bound journalist. So I am indeed an ordained clergyman who is armed, trained and prepared to stop an aggressor even if it means taking a life.

I write with four specific goals in mind:

1) Convince all law enforcement officers, regardless of faith or lack thereof, of the need for ongoing spiritual discernment and practical preparation prior to an incident that requires the use of deadly force.
2) Help law enforcement officers recognize and address any spiritual barriers that may cause hesitation in the use of deadly force.
3) Help law enforcement officers recognize and address the possibility of self-condemnation caused by an incorrect perception of spiritual failure after the use of deadly force where there is a loss of life.
4) Help law enforcement officers in preparing a post-incident personal plan of action.

I would like to begin by addressing some of the words and phrases that I use in this writing. Although I frequently use the word killing, including in the title of this book, it is important to understand the difference between killing and murdering. This is addressed in greater detail in *Chapter Seven*, but while all murder is killing, not all killing is murder. In fact, when it comes to law enforcement officers or even armed citizens using deadly force for the sake of self-defense and/or defense of others, murder is rarely the case. I use the word *kill* for clarification. The word I would prefer to use is *stop*. When a law enforcement officer shoots and kills an aggressor, the intent is not to kill. And this is certainly not murder. The intent is to stop. However, you probably would not be reading this if the title were *Stopping: A Spiritual Discernment Guide for Law Enforcement.*

I also use the phrases *deadly force incident* or *use of deadly force* very often in this writing. I am tempted to use *officer-involved shooting* instead of *deadly force incident*, but this would limit the topic. Without doubt, most of this writing is related to officer-involved shooting incidents, but let's face it, dead is dead regardless of the type of force used. Whether you discharged your firearm or had to use your patrol vehicle as a weapon to stop the aggressor, if the result is death, the issues you will be dealing with will most likely be the same or very similar. The way the use of deadly force affects you may differ greatly from the way it affects your partners, but the type of deadly force used generally does not change the effect and how it impacts you.

An example of this is an officer who was the lead in a vehicle pursuit. In fact, the other officers had not caught up with him as he pursued the suspect's vehicle, so he was essentially alone. When the suspect decided to cross the median and hit a truck head-on, the lead officer in the pursuit witnessed the suspect's rapid and graphic death. Because it was a vehicle pursuit, the death of the suspect was handled much differently than had it been an officer-involved shooting. In fact, it was not even treated as a use-of-deadly-force incident and rightly so. Nevertheless, the officer involved carried a heavy burden. I could see it in his eyes as he kept himself busy working the scene. When I approached him at the scene and asked how he was doing, his response was, "It was just a damn purse!"

This officer had gotten a call of a purse snatched from a

customer while shopping at a local store, had spotted the vehicle that matched the description, and the pursuit was on. In his own way, it seemed that he had taken the responsibility of the suspect's death. If he had just let him get away with that *damn purse*, then this guy would have still been alive. The officer did not say this, but his actions did. About a year after this incident, the officer retired at a rather young age. I do not know if this incident had anything to do with his early retirement, but I believe I personally failed that officer because I never followed up with him about that incident. As a new chaplain at the time, I thought only shootings would have a lasting impact on officers in this way. Like law enforcement training in the academy, chaplain training can also be lacking in certain areas.

While I am certainly approaching this topic from a faith-based perspective, the information contained here can benefit anybody who is willing to utilize it. Whether our faith is strong or weak, or even non-existent, we all have a system of beliefs that impact not only our actions but also our mental and spiritual wellbeing. So although I write from a Judeo-Christian stance, my goal is not to get you to think from the same position. Rather, it is to help you to identify your own stance from your own position. Simply put, your system of beliefs is your business, not mine. My hope is to help you to work through your system of beliefs so that you can be a most proficient law enforcement officer regardless of how our belief systems may or may not clash.

Actually, my job in writing this is much more important than just helping you become a better law enforcement officer. The suggestions I place before you in this writing are intended to help you be a better prepared officer and very well may increase your chances of surviving an incident where you have to utilize deadly force. In fact, following these suggestions may not only increase your chances of surviving, but may also decrease the negative impact that such a life-altering event can have on your life.

You may be thinking, "I don't really need this. I've already come to terms with the possibility of having to kill another person while defending others or myself." And maybe you have. Or maybe you only think you have. After reading this short book and practicing its suggestions, you will obtain some valuable tools to be able to know that you have worked through it. You will never need to second-guess yourself due to lack of spiritual discernment on the topic of killing.

If the time comes for you to deploy deadly force, you will have already identified and dealt with any issues you have, and especially those you didn't know you have, so that 1) you are less likely to hesitate due to an ingrained or even subconscious belief, and 2) if you do have to kill, you won't drag a rotting corpse around with you for the rest of your life due to that same ingrained or subconscious belief.

A friend of mine, Rev. Gavin N. Vaverek, JCL, reviewed and critiqued the first draft of this book. After doing so, he wrote, "A solid discernment about killing can provide a person with conscious preparation to be at peace with the necessary course of action and the consequences of those actions. This book aims to help in this preparation." It is my hope that in this writing you will find my aim to be true and my grouping tight.

<u>INTRODUCTION Source</u>

The Holy Bible. Revised Standard Version, Catholic Edition. Saint Benedict Press, 2009.

HOW TO USE THIS BOOK

This book is separated into two parts. *Part I* provides necessary information and practical steps for you to consider regarding a discernment on killing. I suggest you read every chapter in *Part I* in order to get the most important information from this book. In *Part I* you will learn about discernment and its importance related to being prepared to kill in order to defend self or others. You will also be guided through the discernment process and will be provided a worksheet and checklist to use in your personal discernment. Although the material in this book is copyrighted, I fully expect you to make copies of the worksheet and checklist for your personal use. If you're like me, you do not like writing extensively in a book, especially if you think you may one day share the book with someone else.

Part II contains important information for discernment, but not all chapters in *Part II* will be of interest to all readers. I believe that many will benefit greatly from reading *Part II*, but you may want to use *Part II* as a type of reference section by picking and choosing the chapters you wish to read.

For example, the first chapter of *Part II* walks through my personal discernment on killing. It comes from the viewpoint of a police chaplain who is an ordained Catholic clergyman. This may or may not be of interest to you, but it will give you an example of my struggle and conclusion. It will also help you understand from what perspective I write.

Likewise, there are chapters in *Part II* with information regarding the Catholic Christian, Protestant Christian, and Jewish perspectives on killing in self-defense or in defense of others. You will also find a chapter related to other major religions. Again, these chapters may or may not be of interest to you, but I believe many readers will benefit by reviewing them.

I suggest that all Christians read *Chapter Eleven, Perishing by the Sword: An Answer to Christian Pacifism*, as it will give you food for thought. I also believe that *Chapter Fourteen, The Coward of Broward County?*, will be of interest to most law enforcement officers. Again, use *Part II* as you like, but don't skip *Part I*.

PART
I

CHAPTER ONE

DISCERNMENT ON KILLING

Killing is a life altering event that needs to be discerned before an incident occurs where it becomes necessary to take another person's life. But what exactly is discernment? We are all familiar with decision-making because we all have to make decisions in life. Discernment is a form of decision-making, but it goes deeper, and the answers are more certain as a result. For example, you may ask whether or not you should buy a particular car, or take a particular vacation. You weigh the pros and cons. You talk to your spouse, family or friends about it. And after a while, you come to an answer and act on that answer. This is decision-making.

Discernment is similar but deeper. Discernment should be reserved for truly life-altering actions. In *Part II* of this book, I write that I work with cities and counties as a consultant. For many years, I rented an office space for my business. Month after month I paid rent and after several years I owned nothing but an obligation to pay more rent. I weighed the pros and cons of buying an office building, discussed it with my wife and peers, and made the decision. I also write in *Part II* that I am an ordained permanent deacon in the Catholic Church and that my ordination to the diaconate is for life. I explain that, if my wife dies before I do, I am not allowed to remarry and I would have to live a celibate life. I have vowed to this, but only after much discernment.

The purchase of a property for my business called for decision-making because if I made the wrong decision, we could sell and move back to a rented property. Being ordained, however, called for true discernment because what I was going to do would impact me for the rest of my life and beyond. After promising God that I would serve Him for life, I would not want to say, "Oops, I didn't think about this enough. I change my mind. Never mind God." Decision-making is important for making important decisions, but discernment is crucial for implementing life-altering actions. Discernment on killing is absolutely necessary because, if you are called to take such action, it will certainly be a life-altering event.

Discernment is necessary because, if done right, it uses our system of beliefs to help us understand our position on a particular issue. It forces us to look at who we really are and where we need to be. And this can be difficult. But it is something that we should do for anything that is life-altering important. If you have to use force to the point of killing another human being while defending yourself or others, it will be a life-altering event. It calls for not only decision-making but true discernment as well. Making the right decision to use force, in a fraction of a second, will benefit greatly from your training and your muscle memory. You will not, however, have time in that fraction of a second, to discern this action and the impact it is about to have on your life. And if you pause because you have not done so, you may never have the chance.

Anyone who is engaged in something or considering something that could have lasting effects on their life should engage in discernment prior to taking such action. As a law enforcement officer, you know that every day you go to work, your life could change, or even end on that day. You have come to accept this, but have you truly discerned this? An architect goes to work and knows that during his or her day it is not very likely that a life-altering event will occur at work. But you don't have that luxury. In fact, it is safe to say that you will experience life-altering events during your work, and you should be prepared to deal with these events. If you are not, you may suffer unnecessarily and, most likely, the ones you love will be dragged into your world of suffering.

As many can attest, strange things can happen in the seconds prior to pulling the trigger. Some have tunnel vision, some do not.

Some have an out of the body experience. Some experience time moving in slow motion. Some think of very odd, strange things as they are about to shoot. Some see family members or, more specifically, their children at the moment they are pulling the trigger. And some will doubt the action they are about to take. If you haven't already, please read Lt. Col. Dave Grossman's book, *On Combat*, which goes into great detail about this (Grossman).

There are many reasons for doubt prior to a justified shoot, but none of them are good. You may worry about what pulling the trigger will do to your career. Will you be called a racist or an out of control cop? Will a video of this shooting make it on the news? Or worse, will only a portion of the video, the one that makes you look bad, make it on the news? All of these are concerns that you may have, and you need to deal with them ahead of time. There is training for these and ongoing discussions.

One thought that can enter the mind prior to using deadly force is, "God forgive me," or some variation thereof. This thought can be extremely devastating. Not only can it cause you to hesitate, but unlike many of the other common thoughts that can occur during a use-of-deadly-force incident, it may not go away in the days, weeks or months after the incident. For example, how you will be portrayed on the news may become a non-issue with the next news broadcast. How the incident will impact your career will probably be answered within the next 90 days, if not immediately after. A *no-bill* from the grand jury will end your criminal legal battle. But any thought about God and doubts about how He views your actions may very well linger a lifetime.

Most of us grow up with some kind of religious or spiritual moral influence. It may be as simple as having the Ten Commandments drilled into you. However, most versions of the Ten Commandments are translated as *Thou Shalt Not Kill* instead of *Thou Shalt Not Murder*. It is easy today, sitting in the classroom of "what if", to say that it won't bother you, but reality may be something very different. The mind and our conscience have ways of throwing us curve balls in life. And this doesn't apply only to Christians. Most people of all faiths and even those with no faith have been influenced by their belief systems.

I conducted a random survey of my law enforcement connections on LinkedIn. It was a small survey, only 51 respondents, which is too small to be considered scientific. Nevertheless, it became clear that there is a need for discernment regarding using deadly force. When asked if any class or training during their police academy offered discussions regarding how faith or a system of beliefs may impact or be impacted by the use of deadly force, 80% said the topic was never discussed and 4% said they couldn't recall.

When asked if their department had provided any training that deals with the potential spiritual or emotional impact of using deadly force, 70% said they had received no training in this area and 3% could not recall. When asked if they ever feel concern about how their faith or system of beliefs may conflict with the potential use of deadly force, 61% answered that they have thought about this topic. 65% of the officers stated that they believe they would benefit from a session or training regarding the spiritual or emotional impact of using deadly force and 25% answered *Not Sure*. Some of the ones that answered *Not Sure* offered comments indicating that it would depend on how the session was presented and, if presented right, it could be of benefit.

Eleven of the officers stated that they had used deadly force while on duty, and three of them stated that they had used deadly force more than once. Respondent No. 37 stated that he was on a SWAT team 15 years ago serving a warrant and upon making entry his team was fired upon. Three of the officers were shot and he eventually shot and killed one of the two suspects after a 13-hour standoff. He responded in the survey that in the minutes leading up to the killing of the suspect he did think about his faith and God. He did not hesitate in using deadly force, but he did question how God would view his actions in the days and weeks that followed the incident. He stated that he visited with two priests and one chaplain about the incident and although it's been 15 years since the incident, he still occasionally thinks about how God views his actions, but he doesn't dwell on it.

Respondent No. 22 not only questioned how God viewed his actions after he had to use deadly force, but he commented, "I even went to confession." His comment was referring to the Sacrament of

Reconciliation where Catholics confess sins to a priest and ask God's forgiveness. By going to confession, Respondent No. 22 indicates that even though he was legally justified in using deadly force, he did not believe he was morally justified and therefore sought God's forgiveness. I pray that the priest helped him work through this to see that his actions were not sinful unless he had some impure motive for killing.

Respondent No. 30 shot a suspect during a drug arrest and the suspect survived. When asked, "At any point during the minutes or seconds leading up to the deployment of deadly force, did your faith, morals, or God enter into your mind," he answered, "Not before, but immediately afterward." He stated that after the incident he thought about God's view of him many times, but that it would have been worse if the suspect had died.

Respondent No. 43, however, stated that although he has had to use deadly force four times, he only thought about God in the context of being confident in knowing God. When asked about how God viewed his actions, he stated that he was confident that he and his fellow officers "did God's work." This officer holds a level of conviction that usually comes from some degree of discernment.

In your line of work, there are three areas that truly need to be discerned. In this writing, our focus is on the use of lethal force, discernment on killing. But you also need to discern your exposure to traumatic events and the ongoing trickle of exposure to human depravity. Again, my focus is on using lethal force, taking another life to protect your life or others, but I encourage you to spend time discerning your exposure to traumatic events and the way the people you deal with on a daily basis can negatively impact your outlook on humanity.

There are so many differing opinions on the topic of killing in defense of self or others that I will in no way attempt to cover all of them in this short book. It is important to understand, however, that there is no right or wrong answer to the question of whether or not stopping an aggressor to the point of killing an aggressor is okay *for you*. What is okay for me may not be okay for you. Let me be clear here because I do not want you to think that I have fallen into some kind of relativism. Relativism is defined as "a view that ethical truths depend on the individuals and groups holding them" (Merriam-Webster.com). In other words, relativism says what I hold to be true is true and what you hold to be is true, whether or not they agree, simply because I hold my belief as true and you hold your belief as true. The reality is that truth is truth, period. Either it is or it isn't. Just because I think something is true does not make it so. I reject relativism. Yet even though truth dictates something, our acceptance or rejection of that truth will determine the actions we take, how quickly or delayed we deploy these actions, and how these actions impact our emotional and spiritual well-being in the future. As you will see in *Chapter Seven*, my Catholic faith dictates that killing an aggressor is justified in order to stop the aggressor from killing me or another, but if I don't completely accept that truth, then I certainly should not intentionally place myself in a situation, or career, where I may be faced with making such choices. Yes, we all have the risk of potentially having to defend ourselves, but being a law enforcement officer increases the odds greatly as compared with being in many other professions. And unlike other professionals, law enforcement officers not only have a right to defend self and others, but also a sworn duty. What you are capable of doing may differ from what others are capable of doing.

Likewise, what I am capable of doing may differ from what another clergyman is capable of doing. While I am capable of taking a life in order to save mine or others, a fellow clergyman may not be willing to even consider it. What you are capable of doing as a law enforcement officer may differ from what I am capable of doing as a police chaplain. You leave the comfort of your patrol car to sprint after a filthy, stinky, totally nude male hyped up on PCP and don't hesitate to have full body contact with him in order to stop him from continually exposing himself to the public. I will pray for you and him while you chase him down! Truth for you is that you must chase and truth for me is that I must pray. This is not relativism, but rather understanding where I currently am mentally and spiritually and understanding my duty. The problem arises if the place where I am mentally or spiritually does not allow me to perform my duty.

For example, some law enforcement chaplains see themselves as quasi law enforcement officers. They begin to think that they too have a duty to chase down the bad guy, to help clear a building, to do actual law enforcement. While it may be true that we help in many different ways, we police chaplains usually stay and pray. This is our duty. Yet, if the officer I'm with is taking a beating and I can help, I will. My helping may be radioing for back-up or, if things go far south, I may even need to assist the officer in a physical or possibly violent way. In most cases, however, I'm an observer and my duty will differ greatly from the officer's duty. There are also plenty of law enforcement chaplains who hold a law enforcement commission. Some are full-time law enforcement officers; others are reserve law enforcement officers. I am neither.

If, however, I find myself longing to be a law enforcement officer and begin acting like one, then I will have a problem. First, I will need to recognize my duty as a police chaplain and then recognize that I am longing to be a law enforcement officer. If I am able to see that the two do not match, in my particular case, then I can make changes. I can attend the academy and apply for a law enforcement job. Or I can realize that this is not a reality and adjust my mental desire to be a law enforcement officer. If I am unable to do either of these, then I need to find a different ministry to serve and leave police chaplaincy.

So the truth that we are discussing here is not what is right or wrong and it is not to allow relativism to alter the truth. Rather, it is to make sure that the truth of duty and the truth of mental and spiritual readiness are not in conflict with each other. In fact, the question is not even whether it is right or wrong to kill in self-defense or defense of others. To answer that in different ways and to accept all ways would indeed be relativism. So the question at hand is whether or not *you* consider it to be right or wrong for *you* to kill in self-defense or defense of others.

At this point, you may be tempted to say, "Okay, I can answer that easy question. It's right, not wrong, for me to kill to defend myself, the ones I love, or those to whom I have a sworn duty to protect. Enough said. Time to move on to a different book." However, this is not good enough. It's the lazy way out of a complex question. You should be 100% sure that you have looked at your mental and spiritual readiness to kill ahead of time in order to remove known and unknown barriers.

So when should you begin this discernment process? Yesterday! But since yesterday is already gone, you should begin your discernment immediately and continue it at different points in the future. In other words, it is never too early to discern important issues in your life. But it can be too late.

Many assume that once you discern something, once you have established your conviction regarding a subject, then that's that. You're done. Not quite. You see, truth is truth no matter what. However, how we accept the truth and deal with it may change. For example, God exists and whether or not I accept this truth does not change the truth that God exists. Yet, how I respond to the truth that God exists does change. My faith may grow, or it may weaken. I may come to understand a fuller truth about God, or I may let false statements from others sway my belief. But truth is truth.

So although truth doesn't change when it comes to God, we change and we need to check our beliefs occasionally to make sure our beliefs and convictions are matching our actions. When our actions don't match our convictions, we can have unnecessary issues in many areas of our lives. I suggest that you check your convictions every time you qualify at the range. And if you have any hesitations, any odd thoughts, any doubts, any notable changes in your beliefs, if you changed religions or faiths, or even moved to a different church, or if you've had any major changes or events (divorce, loss of a loved one, change in career, etc.) in your life, then it is probably time to re-discern your position.

Think of it like this: When you get a new firearm, you don't just pull it out of the box and holster it as your duty weapon. Rather, you clean and inspect it, you put many rounds through it, and then you clean and inspect it again. You practice with it and get used to it even if it's the same model you had before. You do this because your life could depend on your sidearm functioning properly and you using it correctly. The same is true for your spiritual and mental well-being. If you have something new going on in your life, you need to review it and make sure that it's not changing your perspective. More specifically, you should make sure that it hasn't impacted your belief system to the point that you have any hesitations in performing your duties.

An example of how our life-experiences can alter our beliefs is found in the story of Bernard B. Kerik. Kerik was the 40th Commissioner of the New York Police Department and was instrumental in cleansing the crime-ridden streets of New York City during the Giuliani years. Yet there is much more to his story. His is a story of personal change.

Kerik was abandoned by his mother when he was a toddler and then raised by his alcoholic father. Although Kerik could have easily wallowed in the true tragedy of his childhood circumstances, and even though he was heading in the wrong direction as a young man, Kerik found love for the martial arts which brought him discipline and determination. His passion for the martial arts, along with his time spent serving our country in the military, eventually helped turn his life in a more positive direction. If you are unfamiliar with his incredible story of success as a law enforcement officer, then pick up a copy of *The Lost Son: A Life in Pursuit of Justice.* You are sure to be inspired as you read about his rise through a highly bureaucratic and political system without a college degree and without special connections.

Through his tenure as NYPD Commissioner, Kerik approached the job with an uncommon balance of fairness and compassion without compromising the stern principles of justice and accountability. The same can be said for his tenure as Commissioner of the New York City Correction Department where he accomplished a near miraculous cleansing of the infamous Riker's Island.

Although Kerik's life story is impressive, he has had many challenges that have formed him and, without doubt, Kerik's positions, opinions, and beliefs have been altered by his life experiences. Most notably is his experience as a federal prisoner. In his book, *From Jailer to Jailed: My Journey from Correction and Police Commissioner to Inmate #84888-054*, Kerik demonstrates how life experiences can change your perspectives and beliefs. Kerik helps the reader understand the changes he experienced and the need for change in our nation's prison system. His book is far from a bleeding-heart writing of liberal mush, but it does offer a perspective that most of us rarely consider. And it is safe to say that Kerik himself probably never thought he would hold such a perspective. In his life movement from law enforcement, to prisoner, and then to top advocate for national criminal justice reform, Kerik demonstrates that life does change us and we would all do well to discern the impacts these changes have on us (Kerik).

When beginning a spiritual discernment on killing, a few key questions should be asked. If you proclaim a particular faith or belief system, how rooted are you in your faith? In other words, is your faith new or relatively new to you, or is your faith the faith in which you were raised? Do you take your faith for granted, and see it as part of your culture, or do you have a renewed calling for your faith, maybe even a renewed zeal for it? Sometimes we grow up in a faith tradition, but it really doesn't become important to us until later in life. And sometimes, the faith we practice now is totally different than the faith we held as a child. Plus many of us were not raised within any particular faith or system of beliefs. Some of us grew up in very religious homes, but are not really participating in any faith now. Your discernment can benefit in considering all of these aspects.

So just how important is your faith or your system of beliefs to you now? In other words, would you change your church community if your spouse said, "Hey, let's try a new church this Sunday?" Would you consider changing your denomination, say from Methodist to Lutheran, or from Baptist to Episcopalian, if you saw something that attracted you to a particular community? What about your religion? If you are Jewish, would you ever consider becoming Christian? If you are Christian, would you ever consider becoming Muslim, or Buddhist, or Hindu? Your answers and the degree of certainty you have in answering is a factor in your current level of faith commitment.

Another important aspect to consider is how often you attend church or other faith-based services. If your shift-schedule is such that you can't make it to church often and are doing good to attend church on Christmas and Easter, then your discernment on killing will probably be a little different than the person who goes to church every Sunday and Wednesday, teaches a Sunday School class, and volunteers at church for special events. If you simply don't attend any services or gatherings because you feel you do not need a church or community in order to connect with God, then your discernment will also likely differ.

Do you think about your faith often, or just when you're at church? In other words, do you pray or read a Bible or other faith-related items often? Do you watch or listen to faith-based shows? If you do this often, then you may have different considerations in your discernment than others.

Other questions to consider are, "What does your faith teach you," and "How well do you know your faith?" When I was growing up, my family didn't really go to church or even talk about God much. So, even though we attended a Baptist church on occasion and then became Episcopalian, I didn't know much about my Christian faith. When I became Catholic, I didn't want to simply believe something just because the priest said so. The Bible has answers, but let's face it, sometimes these answers can be difficult for us to understand. So I decided, as an adult, that if I was going to be Catholic, I had better understand what the Catholic Church teaches and holds to be true. If I had decided to stay Episcopalian, then I would have wanted to understand that system of beliefs. If I had decided that becoming Baptist was the way for me, then I would want to make sure that what that preacher was preaching was true. Seeking the truth can take effort and a lot of discernment.

How well we know our faith is important to how well we practice it, or for that matter, don't practice it. If you are overwhelmed or just don't understand what your faith teaches, then you are probably less likely to follow and practice it. For example, if I preach at Mass using only words like *eschatology* and *Parousia*, then most people won't have a clue of what I'm talking about. But if I preach about the study of the end times and Final Judgment (*eschatology*) and the Second Coming of Jesus (*Parousia*), then most people will understand my preaching. And they are more likely to practice their faith in their daily lives. So if you are sitting through a Sunday service each Sunday and leave with more questions than answers, you will probably not practice what was preached. The more you know about your faith, the easier it is to practice, but there may be more to discern when it comes to killing, or there could be less if your faith is clear and you hold a strong conviction.

Is the knowledge you have about your faith *really* what your faith teaches, or is it just what you *think* your faith teaches you? Very often, the teaching of our faith is not what we think. For example, some in the Catholic Church believe that the Church teaches that everything the Pope says is infallible. So if Pope Francis says something off-the-cuff to a group of reporters while on the airplane, then some may believe this becomes Catholic doctrine or teaching. This is not true, but some Catholics think it is true because they've heard this at some point in their lives, even if it comes from non-Catholics. It is important that you learn what your faith truly teaches and not just what others say it teaches.

What has your family, upbringing, and culture taught you about your faith? How you were brought up influences your faith belief, even if you don't practice the same faith or level of faith as when growing up. For example, let's say you grew up in a devout Seventh Day Adventist family, but now are a practicing Methodist. You may be a Methodist today and having an occasional beer or two is not an issue, but because you grew up as a Seventh Day Adventist, you still find yourself hiding that 12-pack in your grocery cart by covering it with cereal boxes or other groceries as to not been seen with it. As a funny aside, a good friend of mine and his young son stopped by the house one afternoon while I was out in the backyard praying the Evening Prayer. I greeted him with a beer in my hand. Realizing that he is Southern Baptist and that they teach drinking alcohol to be sinful, I pointed out that I was *praying* with a beer. "I know that probably doesn't look right, but I enjoy having a cold beer with God." He responded with a smile. "If I want to have a beer with God, I'll have to go to the next county where nobody will recognize me!"

Another aspect to consider is whether or not the moral teachings you received when growing up or in your culture is truly in line with the faith you now profess? Many Catholics practice some home traditions that do not conform to the teachings of the Catholic Church. This often is due to culture and the lack of understanding the faith. Those born as Catholics occasionally do not follow the teachings of the Church, but rather the teaching of their culture as related to the Church. An example is the statue of Saint Joseph buried upside down in the yard to help sell a house fast. This is nothing but superstition, but some Catholics try this, especially if they are desperate to sell their house. We don't worship statues or images and a plastic version of Saint Joseph buried in my yard will do nothing for me. Yet some Catholics (and some others) do this because they have a friend that says it worked for them and after all, that friend seems to be a really devout Catholic. We do not have to rely on that "really devout Catholic" for truth. And in case you're wondering, the *Catechism of the Catholic Church*, in its treatment of the First Commandment, states, "Superstition is the deviation of religious feeling and of the practices this feeling imposes. It can even affect the worship we offer the true God, e.g., when one attributes an importance in some way magical to certain practices otherwise lawful or necessary. To attribute the efficacy of prayers or of sacramental signs to their mere external performance, apart from the interior dispositions that they demand, is to fall into superstition" (CCC 2111).

Burying a Saint Joseph statue upside-down to sell a house is superstition and a good example of how false teachings creep into the faith we believe. It is up to us to learn what our faith really teaches. There is no Easter Bunny, there is no Santa Clause, and even though we may participate in such festivities, we need to make sure they don't muddle the faith we hold. For me and my faith, I must make sure that my family receives Jesus and not just a secular holiday festival. The same applies to killing in defense. I must hold true to what my faith really teaches me, not what may have been falsely passed down to me from my upbringing, culture or even from a preacher with an agenda.

Have you taken the time to truly consider your personal convictions? If you feel you have little convictions in the areas of faith, then your discernment will take this into consideration, but you should still discern. Maybe you go with the flow when it comes to faith. You'll discern from this viewpoint. But what happens if later in life you gain more convictions regarding your faith, or if you began to grow in faith? You will then need to re-discern your position from this new viewpoint.

What if you have strong convictions and these convictions change? After all, every person grows in understanding, in knowledge, in experience, in wisdom, and hopefully, in faith. Our convictions certainly can change. What if your faith convictions conflict with your duty as a law enforcement officer? This is an important question. In fact, it may be the most important question you can ask. Do my convictions of faith conflict with my duties as a law enforcement officer? What if your faith tradition teaches, "Thou shalt not kill," and they mean that in all cases, no matter the situation or circumstances? The time to ask these questions is now, not after taking lethal action, not after killing someone to protect yourself or others, and certainly not at that very moment when deadly force is needed.

Discernment on killing is vitally important and you will need help in this discernment. Don't go in alone. You need back-up in discernment too! Yes, it is between you and God, but the help of a pastor, chaplain, spiritual friend, or qualified fellow officer is needed. I suggest a pastor over a good spiritual friend because that friend may unknowingly mislead you if he or she doesn't truly know the faith you profess. I then suggest a law enforcement chaplain over a pastor because the chaplain better understands the unique issues associated with law enforcement officers. The chaplain should be able to assist you in your faith or system of beliefs even if he or she does not hold the same faith or beliefs. That's what we are trained to do. I next suggest an armed law enforcement chaplain over an unarmed law enforcement chaplain because the armed chaplain has (hopefully!) engaged in training and discerned the reality that he or she may have to kill. I also suggest a qualified fellow officer over an unarmed chaplain because your fellow officer will understand your issue, but this officer should have a solid spiritual grounding in a faith or system of beliefs similar to yours. I can't stress this enough. You need to have another person or even a group of people to bounce all of this off of in order to make sure you are getting to your true convictions.

You see, I can manipulate my own mind to believe whatever I want. I can look in the mirror and convince myself of the handsome guy that I am. I can also look in the same mirror and convince myself that I'm a slob who nobody likes. When it comes to sin, I can convince myself that doing something is okay. "After all, everybody does it." Or "Hey look there, if he does it then it must be okay." Or "What does it matter, it's not really hurting anybody anyway?"

When I run my thoughts past another person, especially somebody that I respect, then I am less likely to fool myself into a false belief. This person should hold me accountable. But choose wisely! When selecting someone to help direct me, I make sure that I take time to pray to God that He will guide me to the right person. I don't need someone who will tell me what I want to hear, but rather someone who has dealt with similar issues and is grounded in a similar faith and who relies on God for guidance. Again, it is important that we choose wisely.

Think about it this way. No new recruit wants to train under that hard-ass FTO on your shift. But when the training is over and the rookie is on his or her own, they are usually very grateful for the training they received. A soft, lighthearted FTO may be more enjoyable at the time of training, but that same soft, lighthearted FTO may leave you vulnerable to the elements of the job when you hit the streets solo. Pick a hard-ass FTO for spiritual discernment as well and you are much less likely to have significant future issues in this area of your life.

CHAPTER ONE Sources

Grossman, Dave, and Loren W. Christensen. *On Combat: The Psychology and Physiology of Deadly Conflict in War and in Peace.* Warrior Science Pub., 2008.

"Relativism." *Merriam-Webster*, Merriam-Webster, www.merriam-webster.com/dictionary/relativism.

Kerik, Bernard B. *The Lost Son: a Life in Pursuit of Justice.* HarperCollins World, 2002.

Kerik, Bernard B. *From Jailer to Jailed: My Journey from Correction and Police Commissioner to Inmate #84888-054.* Simon & Schuster, 2016.

Catholic Church. *Catechism of the Catholic Church.* 2nd ed. Vatican: Libreria Editrice Vaticana, 2012.

CHAPTER TWO

DISCERNMENT GUIDE AND WORKSHEET

At first glance, the steps and questions below may seem trivial. In fact, the guide and worksheet in a book like this are usually reserved for the end of the book. However, I believe it is so important that you go through these steps that I decided to place this chapter toward the front of the book. More about the importance of these steps can be found throughout the rest of this book, especially in *Part II*.

You can probably answer most of the questions below without hesitation and without much thought or reflection. However, if you want to truly discern the topic of killing, you can benefit from following these steps even if it may seem a waste of time in some areas. The point here is to get you truly contemplating the reality of killing another human being and how it could impact you. In *Chapter Fourteen*, I write that you must address the real possibility that one day you may have to kill. And you should address this reality thoroughly, personally and frequently. By *thoroughly* I mean that it is not good enough to train and prepare physically, but you should train mentally and spiritually as well. By *personally*, I mean that your training should be at a personal level. And *frequently* means not just at a regular training or practice session, but perpetually.

Most people reading this writing will be familiar with the term *muscle memory*. As we practice an action, that action becomes a natural reaction to whatever triggers the action. We train over and over an action and when the time comes to deploy that action, we will react as we have trained. If we train incorrectly, our reaction will most likely be an incorrect action. Our training at the range, for example, should be thorough and all steps must be covered regardless of how mundane they may seem. How many times have you begun training, especially in a team setting, where the range master or instructor reminds you of the basic firearm handling safety rules? You're told over and over and over again to treat all guns as loaded guns, to never point the muzzle at something you're not willing to destroy or someone you're not willing to kill, to keep your finger off the trigger until you're ready to fire, and to be sure of your target and what lies beyond it? You may be a 30-year veteran of law enforcement with countless hours of firearms training, yet you are reminded of these rules (or should be!) at every training session on the range. This is being thorough.

There are a lot of firearms training videos on the market and many of these can be very helpful. However, watching a video that is teaching a draw technique, for example, is far different than being at the range practicing a draw technique with the assistance of an instructor watching you, pointing out your flaws and giving you tips on how to improve. For training to be complete, it should be a personal experience. It should truly impact you.

Finally, in order to improve and solidify our skills, we need to use them frequently. We can practice something over and over and over again in training sessions, but if we rarely practice it again in future training sessions, then we will lose some of that muscle memory that we worked so hard to build. We must practice frequently.

Thorough, personal, and frequent practice builds muscle memory and keeps it in shape. And having a trainer helps you see and work through any flaws you may have so that your muscle memory can fight the *OODA loops* of the world that will be thrown your way. *OODA* is the acronym for *Observe*, *Orient*, *Decide*, and *Act*. Within a split second, you may see a man with a gun (*observe*) and realize that he is pointing it at you while you are standing next to a tree (*orient*), you choose to use that tree as cover (*decide*), and then you move behind the tree while drawing your gun (*act*). The man fires his gun (*observe*) and moves toward you while you are standing behind the tree (*orient*), so you realize that you must stop him (*decide*) and you square your sights, pull the trigger and immediately move off of the "X" (*act*). Your first OODA *loop* in this scenario was slower than your second OODA *loop* because you had to process more new information, but on your second OODA *loop* your muscle memory had already deployed as you began moving behind the tree. The problem is when something unexpected interrupts your OODA *loop*. For example, if the man begins firing as you're taking cover, and then you notice a child standing slightly behind the man, your OODA *loop* will be interrupted with this new information. The same can happen with thoughts. If an unwanted thought jumps into your head at that critical moment, then it can slow down your OODA *loop* or even alter your decision or action (policeone.com). We should address potential unwanted thoughts, the best we can, ahead of time.

So while the questions and steps in the Discernment Worksheet may seem unnecessary, what you are doing is personally and thoroughly addressing the realities in your life, and you should review these questions and steps frequently (every time you qualify at the range) in order to help your muscle memory quickly work through the decision and action part of your OODA *loops*.

Discernment Worksheet

Step 1 – If you are a person of faith, pray to God asking for assistance in the process. If you are Christian, inviting the help of the Holy Spirit is very important. If you are not a person of faith, take time to think and contemplate the importance of this process.

Step 2 – Choose a Spiritual Discernment Assistant (SDA) after asking God to guide you in this decision.

- ☐ Armed Law Enforcement Chaplain
- ☐ Qualified Fellow LEO
- ☐ Unarmed Law Enforcement Chaplain
- ☐ Pastor
- ☐ Spiritual Friend
- ☐ Other

Step 3 – Write down the name and contact information of your SDA.

Contact Information of SDA

____

____

____

Step 4 – Schedule 3 meetings with SDA.

Location, Dates and Times (Max. 1 hour each meeting and at least 1 week apart)

Meeting 1:__________________________________

____

Meeting 2:__________________________________

____

Meeting 3:____

____

Step 5 – Read, pray about or reflect on the questions below and then write down your answers to the following personal inventory questions:

1. Were you raised in a family that practiced a particular faith or particular system of beliefs? (If your answer is *no*, then please write any thoughts or explanations and then skip to Question No. 7.)

2. If so, describe that faith or system of beliefs?

3. Was that faith or system of beliefs practiced regularly, occasionally, or rarely?

4. What did this faith or particular system of beliefs teach regarding killing?

5. Were murder and killing treated differently, considered the same, or just never really addressed?

6. Did you mostly hear the commandment regarding murder as, "Thou Shalt Not Kill" or "Thou Shalt Not Murder" or neither?

7. Are you currently practicing a particular faith or following a particular system of beliefs. (If your answer is *no*, then please write any thoughts or explanations and then skip to Question No. 16.)

8. Is this faith or system of beliefs the same as the faith or system of beliefs in which you were raised?

9. If not, how many years has it been since you began following your current faith or system of beliefs?

10. On a 1 to 10 scale, with 10 being the highest level of importance and 1 the lowest, how important is it to you that you adhere to the teachings of your faith or system of beliefs? Explain why this is so.

11. What does your current faith or system of beliefs teach regarding killing?

12. How sure are you that what you believe is taught by your faith or system of beliefs is actually what it teaches?

13. Does this teaching match your thoughts and opinions regarding killing?

14. If not, does this bother you?

15. Does the teaching of your faith or system of beliefs conflict with the fact that you may have to take a life in order to save your or someone else's life?

16. If you answered *no* to Question 7, then write down a list of what is important to you in life.

Step 6 – Hold Meeting 1 with SDA

Cover the following items during this meeting:

☐ Begin with prayer or greeting.

☐ Discuss your answers to the questions above with your SDA and ask your SDA to share any comments regarding your answers.

☐ If there are any conflicts with the answers above and the possibility that you may have to kill in order to protect, discuss these with your SDA. For example, consider the following:

1. Discuss the difference between "Thou Shalt Not Kill" and "Thou Shalt Not Murder."
2. Discuss differences of a current faith or system of beliefs with the faith or system of beliefs you were taught as a child (if applicable).
3. Discuss how best to address your situation if your faith or system of beliefs teaches pacifism, that killing is wrong under all circumstances.
4. Discuss how best to address your spouse or loved one having a different faith or system of beliefs from your faith or system of beliefs, especially if there are conflicting teachings.
5. Discuss how important (or unimportant) the teachings of your faith or system of beliefs are to you.

Step 7 – Hold Meeting 2 with SDA

Cover the following items during this meeting:

- Begin with prayer or greeting.
- Talk about the reality that you may have to kill in order to stop an aggressor.
- Discuss a scenario where you use deadly force to protect yourself or another person and in which the force you used resulted in the death of the perpetrator. If you have actually had to use deadly force in a past incident that resulted in the death of the aggressor or other person, describe what happened as you answer each of these questions as well as what you believe could happen if you have to use deadly force again.

- Describe what would happen immediately after the incident?
    - Discuss how the department/agency administration would respond.
    - Discuss how your duty weapon would most likely be taken into evidence and how this is standard procedure and would not be an indication that there were negative suspicions regarding your actions.
    - Discuss having a post-incident go-bag (see next chapter).
    - Discuss how you might contact your spouse, family members, or other loved ones to inform them of the incident.
    - Discuss whether or not you have actually talked with your spouse about the possibility of killing and what would follow.
    - Discuss how the legal process may impact your life.
    - Discuss how the departmental policy review may impact your life.
    - Discuss how the media coverage could impact your life.
- If you believe in God, discuss with your SDA how you think God would view you if you had to kill another human being to protect yourself or another person.
- Discuss with your SDA how your family may view you after using deadly force that results in the death of another human being.
- Discuss with your SDA how you would answer the common question asked by children, "Have you ever killed anybody?"

Step 8 – Hold Meeting 3 with SDA

Cover the following items during this meeting:

- Begin with prayer or greeting.
- Discuss with your SDA any reservation or concerns you have regarding the real possibility that you may have to

take life in order to save life.

- Discuss any issues that may have developed or come into light during these sessions, while reading this book, while completing the questions, or while reflecting on the issue of killing.
- With your SDA present, ask yourself if you truly hold the conviction that killing in order to stop an aggressor from harming you or another is a justified action.
- If you believe in God, ask yourself, with your SDA present, if you truly believe that God would support you in your decision to kill in order to stop an aggressor trying to harm you or another.
- If you are unable to offer a solid, affirmative answer to the previous two questions, then discuss a re-evaluation of your career choice as a law enforcement officer with your SDA.

Step 9 – Address any issues or concerns.

- If any issues arise during your meetings with your SDA, or in reading the materials contained here, then it is important that those issues be addressed. If you have been in an incident, pay close attention to your reactions and, if necessary, seek the assistance of a mental health professional. The only shame in having mental health issues is an ongoing practice of ignoring them.

Step 10 – Re-evaluate your convictions.

- Re-evaluate your convictions anytime you have a major change in life.
- Re-evaluate your convictions anytime you change your faith or system of beliefs.
- Review your convictions every time you qualify at the range.

Step 11 – Prepare a Post-Incident Go-Bag

- See *Chapter Three*

CHAPTER TWO Source

"The OODA Loop, Reaction Time, and Decision Making." *PoliceOne*, 23 Feb. 2012, www.policeone.com/use-of-force/articles/5097938-The-OODA-loop-reaction-time-and-decision-making/.

CHAPTER THREE

PREPARING A POST-INCIDENT GO-BAG

Most law enforcement officers have a go-bag filled with items essential to respond to an active attacker. These items often include extra restraining devices, extra ammo, an IFAK (Individual First-Aid Kit) and so on. But when the incident is over and you have just killed another human being, your mind and your body will be in need of stability. The dump of adrenaline from the incident will impact you physically and your mind will not be functioning in a normal manner. A Post-Incident Go-Bag will contain items that will help move you toward stability.

The first item you need in your Post-Incident Go-Bag is a plan of action. By this, I mean an actual written step-by-step plan of action that you can pull from your bag and refer to after the incident. Our department, for example, has written into policy the steps a supervisor takes immediately upon learning of an officer-involved shooting. Your department or agency probably has this in policy also and you need a list of personal planned steps as well. Once you have developed this Personal Post-Incident Plan, make sure your spouse or loved one is familiar with it. In fact, it is even better if you can involve your spouse or loved one in preparing the plan.

A key aspect of this plan is communication with others. I believe it is vitally important that your spouse and/or other loved ones truly comprehend the reality that you may be in a use-of-deadly-force incident and that this will impact you as well as them. Talking about the effects of such an incident after the incident has occurred is not nearly as helpful as talking about the possible effects and preparing for them prior to the incident. DO NOT IGNORE THIS ISSUE! Your well-being and the well-being of your most important relationships could one day depend on a solid understanding of the impacts of a use-of-deadly-force incident. In fact, please read "Section Four: The Price of Combat After the Smoke Clears" found in Lt. Col. Dave Grossman's book, *On Combat*, with your spouse and/or loved ones. You need to understand what to expect and so do they!

Your written Personal Post-Incident Plan should include a list of steps that you need to take while still on scene, immediately after securing the scene and addressing any immediate medical needs. It should also include the steps you need to take after arriving back at the department's station. Finally, you need to have a plan for when you arrive home.

The time to grab your Post-Incident Go-Bag is while on scene, immediately after everything is secure and after the medical needs of all victims, including yourself, as well as the medical needs of the suspect(s) have been or are being addressed. In other words, your Post-Incident Go-Bag needs to be with you while on duty, not sitting in your personal vehicle back at the station.

Your Personal Post-Incident Plan should begin with some practical reminders. More than likely, your training has kicked in and you have already begun the calming process of combat breathing. There are different variations of this, but a common version of combat breathing is to breathe in through your nose while counting 1 to 4, hold that breath for another count of 1 to 4, exhale through your mouth while counting 1 to 4, hold the exhaled breath while counting 1 to 4, then repeat all steps several times. If you haven't begun this, your Personal Post-Incident Plan will remind you of it.

It will also remind you to invoke silence. Your world has just been turned upside down. Your adrenaline has dumped. Your mind is spinning. Body cameras are recording. Even if you and everybody around you know that your use of deadly force was 100% justified, it is completely natural to want to defend these actions. "He was coming at me!" This simple statement of how you immediately recall the actions of the suspect could be used against you if the jury sees anything less than the suspect moving full charge aggressively toward you. You were there, your sixth sense kicked in, you had a history with this guy, you knew what he was capable of, and when he took that one flinch toward you with knife in hand, you knew he was coming at you. You took the right action in stopping him. However, his family's attorney might say something like, "On video, immediately after you killed Bob, you clearly said he was coming at you. But as we see, Bob only made one little movement. How do you know he was coming at you?"

It is also a common reaction to display anger or aggression right after a high-stress incident. "I got the M-F-er!" When the family's attorney sees that little video clip, he'll think Christmas came early. So stay silent because you never know what may come from your mouth immediately after a high-stress incident. Just concentrate on your breathing and let the other officers take over and your supervisors guide you. And only say what is immediately necessary or required.

Next, drink a bottle of water and call your spouse or loved one. Since you're still on scene, the only message you need to relay is that you are okay. You can talk more about the incident later, but right now your well-being is all that needs to be communicated. This is an extremely important step that should not be skipped. News in today's world is almost instantaneous and you do not want your spouse or loved ones learning about a shooting through social media. The wife of an officer, for example, can be messaging on Facebook with a friend when another friend messages that there's been an officer-involved shooting at the mall. She asks which mall and the friend provides the name of the mall, which happens to be in her husband's district. She goes to a local television station's website and reads the headline, "Officer involved in shooting at local mall. Two people confirmed dead." She calls her husband and he does not answer. If you happen to be that husband, there's no need to let her go through that anguish. Call, or even text her and let her know you are okay as soon as you get the chance. This is a good practice even if you are not part of the incident and it happens on your beat.

When you get back to the station, ask your supervisor if you can change out of uniform and into your normal street clothes. Sometimes pictures need to be taken, so make sure to ask before you change or clean yourself up. But as soon as you are allowed, go ahead and put on some street clothes. If you were just involved in an officer-involved shooting or other type of similar incident that resulted in a fatality or even serious injury, your patrol duty for the night is over and, more than likely, you're going to be there for a while. You may have, possibly without noticing it, soiled your clothes during the incident. A loss of bowel or bladder control is not uncommon in an extremely high-stress situation and is not a sign of weakness or of being cowardly (Grossman). So have a change of clothes available. Plus, getting comfortable is a step toward getting back to normal.

As soon as possible, call your legal representative and do exactly as he or she says. If you have just killed someone, there will be investigations and the investigations will not be easy. You can make it much more difficult than it needs to be by ignoring the council of your legal representative. So follow all instructions closely. The only exception to this is if your legal advisor tells you not to call your spouse or loved one, especially if you weren't able to do so at the scene. This second call is important because the fact that you have left the scene and arrived at the station will convey a comforting message to your spouse that you are safe and clearly out of harm's way. This call from the station should be a voice call and not a text message. Your spouse needs to hear your voice to really know that you are okay. If you've already called your spouse to tell him or her that you are okay, they will want to know more details, but you will probably not be able to say much at this point. This can be very distressing to your spouse. He or she may wonder why you are excluding him or her from this very important incident in your life. Talk about this ahead of time and make sure your spouse understands that you will be under both criminal and departmental investigations, even if your use of deadly force is clearly justified. Make sure he or she understands that this is procedure no matter who the involved officer is or the circumstances. From chief to rookie, the procedure is (or should be!) the same. And if possible, have a plan for your spouse to have support while all of this is happening. Your spouse sitting at home, alone, worrying about you and having little-to-no information can be very traumatic. If at all possible, have the spouse of a fellow officer who your spouse knows engage with your spouse during these hours after the incident prior to your return home. While finalizing my first draft of this writing, our department had an officer-involved shooting incident and the wife of the officer involved was somewhat upset with him for not providing her with much information. A fellow officer had gone through the experience that follows an officer-involved shooting the previous year, so he asked his wife to reach out to this officer's wife. This helped greatly in calming the concerns of the officer's wife.

In many cases, it is advisable for your spouse or loved one to join you at the station for support. This may or may not be permissible depending on your department's policy. If it is permissible and if you have children, have a plan of who will watch them if it's 2 o'clock in the morning when the incident occurs.

After you've contacted your spouse this second time, try to eat a snack, especially if it's been a while since you've eaten or if you vomited away the meal you did eat (this too is not uncommon). And drink some more water. If a department chaplain has not been called, request one. This is especially important if you have been gagged by legal or by your administration and are unable to talk about the incident to anyone. A chaplain can offer confidentiality in which you can share information about the incident in order to help the healing process begin. You will also be given the opportunity to meet with someone in the mental health field. Hopefully, this will even be required. Receive this opportunity with open arms when the time comes. But for now, while at the station, ask for a chaplain. And if today you do not know your department chaplain, get to know him or her. It helps to see your chaplain as a friend or brother in blue. A chaplain visiting with you for the first time ever will be much less useful than a chaplain you already know.

If a chaplain is not available or if you haven't gotten to know one of your department chaplains, then consider contacting your Spiritual Discernment Assistant (SDA). Just keep in mind that your

SDA may or may not be able to offer the same level of confidentiality offered by a chaplain.

Once at home, you need to take care of yourself physically and mentally. Exercise, take a shower, eat a decent meal, and get some rest. Wind down with prayer or, if you're not a person of faith, some form of peaceful relaxation. If your mind is going ninety-to-nothing, start reading Grossman's *On Combat*. This is also a time to avoid alcohol or unnecessary medication. There's little I enjoy more after a difficult day than sitting outside and sipping on a cold bottle of Shiner Bock beer. You too may be tempted to have a cold beer in order to relax after this difficult day. Don't. Save it for another time. The day you just had is much more than just *a difficult day*.

You could have difficulty sleeping, but turning to alcohol is not the solution you need. A study by the National Institute of Justice shows that 46% of officers had difficulty sleeping during the first 24 hours following an officer-involved shooting and 36% had difficulty sleeping throughout the first week following the incident. This percentage drops to 16% over the first three months after the incident and then to 11% after three months (nij.gov). Alcohol use can help you get to a deep sleep quickly, but it also causes you to skip the REM (rapid eye movement) sleep stage. As the effects of the alcohol begin to diminish, you can fall into REM sleep. It is easy to wake up while in the REM sleep stage and once you're awake, it may be very difficult to get back to sleep (adrenalfatiguesolution.com). It can become a vicious cycle.

If you can't sleep, pull out your journal and write. What?! You don't have a journal? Of course you don't! Most of us don't have time for that kind of mumbo-jumbo. And who in the world wants to write down the garbage you have to deal with on a daily basis? Right? Well, it's a good time to make a change. You've just been through an experience that is going to change you to some degree. Writing down the events and your thoughts regarding the experience is very therapeutic. Doing this will help you clear your mind, de-stress, improve your memory, and begin healing. It also fosters overall self-improvement (forbes.com). Hopefully, you will not have yet given your official statement, so writing about the incident after you get home will help you offer your statement in clarity when the time comes.

It's a good idea to begin a journaling session with prayer. Invite the Holy Spirit to help you see clearly what you need to see and to guide you in your writing. If you are not a person of faith, then try to get relaxed and get into the proper mental state for this endeavor. Your journal should be written in secrecy and only for your eyes. Do not write with the intent of sharing it with others. Some may disagree with me on this, but if you write with the intent of sharing, you are more likely to write in a way that you think will influence the person's opinion of you or the incident. Write for yourself and yourself alone and let truth be truth (truth of the incident, truth of your actions, truth of your thoughts and feelings, etc.). If you're worried about someone else reading it, then burn it after you've written it.

In whatever way this event impacts you, monitor your reactions closely. Turn a negative action into a positive one. Want a beer? Have a glass of refreshing water instead; your body needs this. Want to order a Ray's Pizza and pig out while binge-watching some mind-numbing series on Netflix, fix a healthy meal and exercise instead; your body needs this. Feel angry and want to yell at anybody who looks at you the wrong way, find a quiet place and yell at God. He can take it. Then talk to Him and allow Him to guide you as you sit in silence; your soul needs this.

Whatever you do, make sure you have a plan in place ahead of time. Print your Personal Post-Incident Plan and place it in your Post-Incident Go-bag.

Your Post-Incident Go-Bag will contain the following items:

1. A copy of your written Personal Post-Incident Plan.
2. List of important phone numbers (even those you know by memory).
3. A **full** set of street clothes - underwear, shirt, pants, belt, socks, shoes, etc.
4. At least three bottles of water.
5. Energy/Protein Bar
6. Copy of Lt. Col. Dave Grossman's book, *On Combat*, with Section 2 and Section 4 bookmarked or dog-eared.

7. Notebook and pen.

Here is an example of how a Personal Post-Incident Plan can look:

Personal Post-Incident Plan

Immediately After Incident - Still on Scene - with Scene Secure

1. If you haven't already, begin your combat breathing exercise.
    a. Breathe in through nose, 1...2...3...4...
    b. Hold, 1...2...3...4...
    c. Breathe out through mouth, 1...2...3...4...
    d. Hold, 1...2...3...4...
    e. Repeat
2. Hush! Say only what is immediately necessary or required.
3. Drink a bottle of water.
4. Call spouse or loved one and tell him/her
    a. that you are okay,
    b. that you have been involved in an incident,
    c. that you will call later with more details, and
    d. that you *really* are okay.

Once Back at Station

5. Change into street clothes.
6. Drink another bottle of water.
7. Find a private location to make phone calls.
8. Call legal representative and follow all instruction.
9. Call spouse or loved one again. If legal says not to call, call anyway!
    a. Tell him/her as much or as little as you want, in private, and reminding him/her not to share any information about the incident with anyone.
    b. If spouse is going to come to the station and there are minor children involved, make sure there is a plan for somebody else to watch them.
10. Drink another bottle of water and eat a small snack.
11. Call your SDA (see Chapter Two) or a chaplain if one hasn't already been called.

At Home

12. Drink another bottle of water.
13. Exercise for 20-30 minutes.
14. Shower.
15. Eat full meal if hungry or a small snack if not hungry.
16. Wind down with prayer, relaxation or begin reading *On Combat*.
17. Do not drink alcohol, use drugs, or take medications other than as prescribed.
18. Sleep
19. If you can't sleep, write or read.

CHAPTER THREE Sources

Grossman, Dave, and Loren W. Christensen. *On Combat: The Psychology and Physiology of Deadly Conflict in War and in Peace.* Warrior Science Pub., 2008.

"Police Responses to Officer-Involved Shootings." *National Institute of Justice*, nij.gov/journals/253/pages/responses.aspx.

Taylor, Tracy, and Arnold. "Should You Avoid Alcohol If You Have Adrenal Fatigue?" *Adrenal Fatigue Solution*, 1 Jan. 2017, adrenalfatiguesolution.com/alcohol-adrenal-fatigue/.

Nazish, Noma. "Five Reasons To Keep A Journal In 2018." *Forbes*, Forbes Magazine, 10 Jan. 2018, www.forbes.com/sites/nomanazish/2017/12/29/five-legit-reasons-to-keep-a-journal-in-2018/#523905dd55e1.

CHAPTER FOUR

ARE YOU PREPARED? REALLY?

The late Jeff Cooper, a retired colonel of the Marines who served in the Pacific during World War II and in clandestine operations during the Korean War (americanrifleman.org), is known for his color codes of situational awareness. He taught that *Condition White* is when a person is in the most relaxed and unaware state, *Condition Yellow* is when a person is relaxed but very aware of what surrounds them, *Condition Orange* is when a person has noticed something or someone that may or may not be of concern, and *Condition Red* is when a person has determined that something or someone is of enough concern to begin investigating and readying themselves to respond appropriately. Some, including Massad Ayoob, author, tactical trainer of law enforcement officers and civilians, and all-around gun guru, have added *Condition Black* as the state in when use-of-force action is actually being taken (Ayoob). For law enforcement officers, being in *Condition White* while being awake is simply unacceptable (policeone.com). I realize that this is an oversimplification of Cooper's color coding, and I also realize that there are other interpretations of these codes as well as expansions. However, I would like to focus mostly on *Condition Yellow* in this chapter.

In Cooper's *Condition Yellow*, you are aware of where you are, who and what surrounds you, where you can find concealment, where you can take cover, and, if necessary, how you can escape or get your family to safety. Although you may have good situational awareness while in *Condition Yellow*, are you prepared to move into *Condition Orange* and *Condition Red?* If you have not prepared yourself to move into *Condition Orange* and *Condition Red*, then you may never get there. Let me explain.

Condition Orange is when you notice something or someone that could cause concern. If you don't possess the proper mental and spiritual preparedness, you may not reach *Condition Orange* because you simply do not accept the potential for threat. In other words, you were not in a true *Condition Yellow*. Here's an example: Your next-door neighbor has invited your family and a few other neighborhood families over to watch the big game. It's your day off, you know all of the families invited, and you enjoy their company. So you're in. You prepare the 7-layer bean-dip that you agreed to bring and off you go.

When your family arrives, you greet the other neighbors, grab a drink, and settle in for the game. One of the neighbors has brought his sister and brother-in-law with them who are visiting from out of State. You do not know them, but they seem nice enough. As the evening goes by, everyone is actively watching the game, which is very close in score, while the kids are playing rather loudly in a bedroom upstairs. The visiting couple retreated to the kitchen after a short disagreement about something unimportant and they haven't been seen since in the last quarter, but you're really not paying attention to them. The score is tied, your team is about to score and there is now less than 10-seconds left in the game. You hear a dish crash to the floor in the kitchen and the host hops up to investigate. Your team begins their play and the game is immediately stopped for a penalty. Just as the play resumes, another sound comes from the kitchen, this time a little muffled. Or maybe it was just the kids upstairs. Three seconds are left in the game and this is the final play.

You never move from *Condition Yellow* to *Condition Orange* because you are comfortable and complacent with this familiar setting. In fact, your off-duty weapon sits safely in your safe next door. Why? Because you are not prepared. You have actually been moving back and forth between *Condition Yellow* and *Condition White*. So when shots ring out from the kitchen, and the ball is snapped, and the kids bang something upstairs, and your drink spills, you are frozen not by fear, but by a brain that is trying to process it all.

Moving from *Condition Yellow* to *Condition Orange* and then on to *Condition Red* takes being prepared to be aware. You should be mentally and spiritually prepared to consider all possibilities. It is not paranoia to maintain *Condition Yellow* and to enter into *Condition Orange* when something just doesn't seem right. But you are very unlikely to notice when things *just don't seem right* if you are bouncing into *Condition White*. Being unprepared, in my opinion, is just as bad as being what some consider a sheep grazing around in *Condition White*.

Being prepared takes more than just being trained and being armed. It also takes a mental and spiritual willingness to act. As has been discussed in previous chapters, you should remove any possibility that your faith or system of beliefs conflicts with your resolve to respond to violence with violence. But it doesn't stop there.

Not only should these conflicts be removed, but you would also be well served by a mental preparedness to *act*. A good practice is to run mental *what-if* scenarios wherever you are on an ongoing basis. In the example above, had the off-duty officer run mental scenarios, he probably would not have predicted exactly what actually happens. However, running scenarios in his mind would have helped him realize that he was not prepared (firearm at home in safe), that he was not paying attention to the factors that surround him (visiting couples who are strangers to him, have dispute, have been in kitchen for a long time, something being broken, etc.) and that he was acting like a complacent sheep (munching on snacks in a familiar, seemingly safe setting).

Even more importantly, taking the time to run these mental scenarios and actually visualizing what a situation might look like helps prepare you for harsh realities should an incident occur. In my study of Broward County SRO, Scot Peterson, I'm pretty much convinced that he froze in place because he was overwhelmed with a reality that he truly had not considered. He may have known a school shooting was possible, but I don't think he had pictured it in reality at *his* school and happening to *his* students. You can read more about that in *Chapter Fourteen*.

I believe the key to successful scenarios is to make them personal and detailed. Simply running a mental scenario of a man shooting at another officer, for example, is not enough. See the man, see the officer, know the officer, see it in a very familiar location, even a location where you feel the safest, and see it ending in the worst outcome possible. A scenario of you stopping a suspect from shooting your partner is good. A better practice is you attempting to stop the suspect, your partner getting hit, and now you alone with the suspect who is focusing all his rage on you. Shoot! Fight! Do whatever you have to do to live! See in your mind's eye what it looks like to fail and then be on your last leg fighting to the end. Feel the pain of your life slipping away from your children's future. Fail. Fight. Feel the fear of facing God for your final judgment. Are you ready for that right now? Fail. Fight. Some may disagree with me on this stating that if you envision the win, you are more likely to win. Some people use a picture of their dream house or car to help them achieve their goal of winning. But that is a car or house or stuff. What we're discussing is your life and the life of your family. So I offer this strategy with logic. If you always run mental scenarios where you always win, where you always take out the bad guy, then you set yourself up for a mental freeze if it doesn't work out that way. No freeze is allowed! You have to stay in the fight to the bitter end, no matter what! So fail and then fight!

The next time you are in a familiar place that you consider a refuge or a safe place to be, run scenarios. Sitting in the breakroom at your station surrounded by LEO family is a place where your guard may be down. After all, you're deep in the station, in a secure area, with little-to-no visitors. Run a mental scenario anyway. Someone gets in, or even better, a fellow officer snaps. I know this sounds unnecessary, maybe even silly, but if you do this on a regular basis, I believe you will be less likely to freeze up with a brain that is trying to disseminate the unthinkable.

Likewise, your family should also be familiar with scenarios to some degree. This was touched upon in *Chapter Three*, but I can't stress enough the importance of fully understanding how an officer-involved shooting or other use of deadly force incident can change your life. Not only can your marriage be strained by the events that happen after the incident, but your marriage may also be negatively impacted by how the incident affects you mentally, emotionally, and spiritually. So discuss with them the possibilities and even offer scenarios so they will know what to expect. Think of it this way: The time to address a problem is before the problem occurs. You can lessen the strain by addressing potential issues in advance. For example, if you know you're going to be short financially this month, the best action is to discuss this with your spouse and to begin working on a solution together. Waiting until the lights are shut off to address the issue is a recipe for marital disaster. So use scenarios of use-of-force incidents to explain how all of this may look and how the investigations may be handled in your department. Use scenarios to demonstrate how the news media and social media may twist reality. In fact, there's no shortage of real-life cases that you can discuss with them where an officer did his or her duty and then was crucified in the court of public opinion.

As you know, when your marriage is negatively impacted, your children and other loved ones can also be negatively impacted by the incident. But this is only part of the issue. The people who make up the society in which you surround yourself may, knowingly or unknowingly, alter the way they act around you and your family. They may treat you differently, maybe even coldly. Of special concern will be your children. Other children at school or church may have heard about the incident and want to discuss it with your children. They could approach your children and ask innocent questions out of curiosity. Or they may have heard negative things about the incident and use this to make fun of or bully your children. I strongly suggest that as soon as your children reach an age of reason, you discuss with them some of what your job entails and the potential that you may have to kill in order to save the lives of others or yourself. This will not be an easy discussion and only you can decide how much or how little and in how much detail should be discussed with your children. If an incident occurs, I also suggest that you discuss with them the events and provide them with as much defensive information as you think they can handle. Ayoob put it this way, "If you are not prepared for some of these sociological manifestations in the aftermath, they can tear you and your family apart. Divorce rates and other family estrangements run high after you've been forced to shoot in self-defense" (Ayoob). Please address this now before it's too late. You do not want to become another one of those negative statistics.

So not only should you be prepared, but allow your family to be in a type of *Condition Yellow* as well. They need to be aware of what life could look like after an officer-involved shooting or other similar incident. They need to know what may happen and where to find the appropriate help, be it legal, financial, mental or spiritual. Ask yourself these questions: *If I had to kill another person right now to save my life or the life of another, would my family know what to expect? Am I sure that I fully understand what to expect? Am I prepared?*

CHAPTER FOUR Sources

Ayoob, Massad F. *COMBAT SHOOTING with Massad Ayoob.* Gun Digest Books, An Imprint of F W Media, Inc., 2011.

"Throwback Thursday: Jeff Cooper." *American Rifleman*, www.americanrifleman.org/articles/2015/3/26/throwback-thursday-jeff-cooper/.

"Cooper's Colors: A Simple System for Situational Awareness." *PoliceOne*, 9 Aug. 2010, www.policeone.com/police-trainers/articles/2188253-Coopers-colors-A-simple-system-for-situational-awareness/.

CHAPTER FIVE

THE IMPORTANCE OF A CHAPLAINCY PROGRAM

I'm a police chaplain, so of course, I'm going to tell you that it is important for your department or agency to have a chaplaincy program. But don't let my biased opinion convince you. Let's look at what others have to say.

The president of the National Association of Chiefs of Police, Jack L. Rinchich, supports and encourages all police departments to have a chaplain program. He writes, "The primary role of the police chaplain is to provide spiritual support, insight, and encouragement to officers who seek help. They also can set the tone for departments by demonstrating moral conduct, compassion, and decency. In many cases the chaplain simply is a shoulder to cry on or a listening ear. It takes time for them to gain the confidence and trust of police officers because some officers can be cynical, paranoid, or resistant to anything with a religious tone."

With time, however, and with trained chaplains who understand that their role in the department is to provide spiritual support and not to proselytize, many officers come to see the chaplains as true resources in helping meet their personal needs. According to Rinchich, "Police chaplains serve in a variety of ways, such as performing marriages, assisting with line-of-duty deaths, participating in ceremonial functions, speaking at churches and community organizations, presenting awards, visiting hospital patients, providing spiritual guidance and moral support, and developing police chaplaincy programs. Departments with chaplains are fortunate because they provide vital services not only to the agency but also to the local community."

Chaplains are not called to be visitors of the department, but rather to become part of the department. As the chaplain begins to experience much of what the officers' experience, he or she becomes a member of the family in blue. Rinchich writes, "Chaplains confront numerous difficult situations, such as deterring bridge jumpers and suicidal individuals who often are armed, delivering death notifications to family members, praying over dying officers, and providing comfort and spiritual support to countless people and distressed victims. The most challenging incidents are those in which fellow officers are killed in the line of duty, threaten suicide, struggle with family breakups, agonize over rebellious or wayward children, battle drug addiction, or wrestle with financial problems. People often forget that law enforcement officers are human beings with the same passions and struggles as everyone else" (leb.fbi.gov).

Although some law enforcement chaplains are also licensed to practice mental health treatment, most are not and offer a separate, necessary service that most of the time cannot be filled by a department psychologist. "In past years, some police departments have turned to police psychologists to counsel officers in need. In many cases, they perform important functions that work hand-in-hand with what chaplains do. However, chaplains offer a different kind of emotional support. Officers aren't going to feel comfortable confiding in a psychologist who takes notes and keeps the information on file. Often the only contact officers have with a staff psychologist is in their office and after a crisis situation. No rapport or relationship has been established, and the information usually can be found in an officer's personnel file. Whatever is shared with a chaplain is confidential and goes no further" (policemag.com).

The *Chaplain Resource Manual* prepared by the National Sheriffs' Association states, "An effective chaplaincy program should be an integral part of any sheriff's office. This program can take many different forms in order to conform to need, resources, and capabilities within the community and organization. Many sheriffs' offices utilize chaplaincy volunteer programs." Chaplains play many different roles with the departments they serve. For example, the manual states, "When a hostage is taken, the chaplain should be dispatched." While chaplains are not normally involved in negotiations with hostage takers or barricaded subjects, they can play an important role between the inner perimeter where SWAT and negotiators are staged and the outer perimeter where the public and press may be held. Chaplains can provide support along with limited information to the family and public, much like the public information officer works to relay information to the press. Although the chaplain can be of help with the family and public in such situations, the primary focus of concern will always be with the officers on scene.

I try to convey to the officers I'm with that I am there for them. I will assist with the needs of the public, but only if those needs benefit the officer and his or her duty. I am there for them, first and foremost. The Sheriffs' Association explains, "The type of people and criminal actions law enforcement encounter in communities and jails can sometimes be shocking. This emotes feelings the average person is very often not equipped to process alone. As a community oriented profession, we train law enforcement not to disclose feelings at such incidents. The nature of the profession asks that feelings and normal reactions to the extraordinary be put aside. This can result in higher rates of alcoholism, drug abuse, divorce, and, sometimes, suicide. In a service profession to law enforcement, as well as to the incarcerated, and former inmates, the chaplain has a unique perspective of, and possibly is better equipped to address basic problematic events and emotions" (sheriffs.org).

Although I strongly suggest the implementation of a chaplaincy program for your department if you do not already have one, I do not suggest this if the department is not willing and able to make sure a clear chaplain policy is in place, the chaplains chosen are rigorously screened, and the chaplains are adequately and regularly trained. Without these three aspects of a chaplaincy program, it could end up doing much harm to your department as well as the department's relationship with the community you serve.

In addition, it is important that the role of law enforcement chaplains be clearly defined as providing support for the members of the department they serve. While chaplains may be able to provide support to the community, the officers need to know that when push comes to shove and members of the community turn against them, the chaplains have their backs. To address any concern or division of roles that the chaplains may face, consider implementing a clergy and police alliance program. A clergy and police alliance can provide a bridge between the department and the community. There are many successful models for this around the country and your chaplains can certainly help you in developing this program.

The most recognized organization of law enforcement chaplains is the International Conference of Police Chaplains (ICPC). ICPC provides several regional training seminars around the country, and internationally, as well as an annual training conference. The ICPC website states that it is:

- *An international, professional membership organization made up of chaplains and liaison officers from different faith groups and law enforcement agencies.*
- *A training and equipping organization to assist individual chaplains and/or their departments.*
- *An organization that allows an individual's ministry to be expanded and expressed in a new way.*
- *An organization that assists in the starting of chaplaincy programs or strengthens existing programs.*
- *An organization offering professional training levels to chaplains of different and varying levels of experience.*
- *An organization that encourages and fosters networking between chaplains.*
- *An organization that seeks partnerships with other professional organizations and chaplaincy groups.*
- *An organization that expresses itself with religious tolerance and respect for people of all faith traditions or no faith tradition.*
- *An organization that provides a safe-haven for wounded chaplains.*
- *An organization that has a world-vision for chaplaincy.*

Likewise, ICPC makes it clear that it is not:

- *An extension of [the chaplain's] denomination or faith group*

- *A Christian-only organization*
- *A "certifying" agency*
- *An ecclesiastical endorsing or licensing entity*
- *A place to build a resume*
- *A clique, club, or private organization*

There are other organizations that do a fine job in providing training and other resources for chaplains. Whatever path your department chooses, make sure that your chaplains are trained and formed in the field of law enforcement chaplaincy. Just because someone has twenty years experience pastoring a large church doesn't mean that they have what it takes to serve in this unique capacity (icpc4cops.org).

Many departments have policies that prevent chaplains from being armed. I believe this is a mistake. I say this not only because I believe chaplains should be able to defend themselves and even defend others while serving your department, but I also believe a policy of unarmed chaplains sends an unintended message. You see, if we say that chaplains in the military and in law enforcement should not be armed because of their clerical status and/or pastoral duty, or because they have a higher calling, then we send a message that in order to be holy, or truly right with God, we should put down our weapons. As you will read in *Chapter Eleven*, Jesus never commanded us to put down the sword, but rather to put it in its place. For a chaplain, the sword has its place. The chaplain's firearm, if that chaplain chooses to be armed, should be used only as a means for self-defense or defense of others. It should not be used for law enforcement since the chaplain is normally not engaged in enforcing the law. I strongly suggest that your department offer chaplains appropriate training, and if there is a legal avenue in your state to allow for it, they be allowed to be armed if they so desire.

CHAPTER FIVE Sources

"Officer Wellness Spotlight: Police Chaplains - An Integral Part of Law Enforcement." *FBI*, FBI, 9 Dec. 2015, leb.fbi.gov/spotlights/officer-wellness-spotlight-police-chaplains-an-integral-part-of-law-enforcement.

"Police Chaplains: Helping Hands." *Police Magazine*, www.policemag.com/channel/patrol/articles/1996/02/helping-hands/page/2.aspx.

"Chaplains Reference Guide." *National Sheriffs' Association*. https://www.sheriffs.org/sites/default/files/tb/ChaplainsResource Manual.pdf

"International Conference of Police Chaplains - Serving All Law Enforcement Chaplains - ICPC Is/Isn't." *International Conference of Police Chaplains - Serving All Law Enforcement Chaplains -* ICPC Video, www.icpc4cops.org/about-us/what-we-do/icpc-is-isnt.html.

CHAPTER SIX

BLUE-ON-BLUE OFFICER-INVOLVED SHOOTINGS

The main purpose of this book is to convince you of the need to truly discern the fact that you may have to kill another human being in the line of duty or even when off-duty while protecting yourself or others and to give you some tools to help you complete this discernment. However, no amount of discernment will eliminate the tragedy of accidentally killing a fellow officer or other innocent individual due to mistaking him or her as a suspect. The only way I can help you in that area is to stress the importance of being able to clearly identify your target prior to using deadly force. In addition, I want to stress how very important it is that you clearly identify yourself as law enforcement, especially when you are off-duty or in plainclothes.

According to the 2010 Harvard sponsored report, *Reducing Inherent Danger: Report of the Task Force on Police-on-Police Shootings,* from 1986 to 2009, there were 26 police officers in the United States killed by other police officers because they mistakenly thought they were the suspects. The report states that scholars reported that "two categories of officers—those working undercover or in plainclothes—were the most likely to have weapons drawn on them or otherwise to be involved in 'near-miss' confrontations" due to uniformed officers mistaking them for suspects. It also states, "For off-duty officers who draw their weapons to take police action, these confrontations may be more dangerous. This is especially the case if they are off-duty in places where they do not normally work and are therefore unlikely to be recognized by local officers. In many agencies, officers are unlikely to have received training, except perhaps briefly when they first join the police or at the firing range, on how to take action off-duty and then how to respond when they are confronted by a uniformed officer" (harvard.edu).

The training offered by Texas State University's Advanced Law Enforcement Rapid Response Training (ALERRT), which is discussed in *Chapter Fourteen*, stresses the importance of conducting a *scanning sequence* in order to determine if a particular person is a threat. "First responders must train to mechanically search through and see what is pertinent." ALERRT teaches that you should begin with a quick scan of the entire person. Do you know the person? Is the person displaying anything that visibly identifies that person, such as a uniform, badge, or identification? What is the person's posture or how is the person moving? Next, a scan of the hands is needed. ALERRT reminds the student, "Hands kill." Is the person holding any weapon? What about the waste line? Most criminals tuck weapons in their belt or pants instead of using holsters. "Scanning the entire person and the hands are the most critical and when done properly will take only a fraction of a second to make sure your decision is right."

What about the area immediately around the person? Is a weapon close by? What does the person's demeanor suggest? Is he complying with commands? "A systematic scanning sequence of a person can be critical in the prevention not only of using deadly force against a legally armed citizen who is attempting to stop an active shooter, but also can prevent the shooting of an off-duty or plain clothes officer as well" (Texas State University 22-25).

There are products available to help identify off-duty and plainclothes officers. The Don't Shoot Me safety banner from DSM Safety Products has been around for a few years. It is a highly effective visual identifier that is worn across the torso and back by off-duty and plainclothes officers responding to active incidents. It is kept in a pouch worn on the belt and the officer pulls it out and over the shoulder like a sash in order to deploy it. The sash is yellow with an identifying word, such as *POLICE* or *SECURITY*, written across it in reflective silver (dsmsafety.com).

Another good product is a small hat that is commonly referred to as the *Israeli cap*. This little cap folds into your pocket and you pull it out and wear it when needed. It is dark blue in color with an identifier, such as *POLICE* or *CCW* printed in blue across a white patch (Cherries).

My favorite identifier, by far, is the Armed ID arm banner. I must admit that I am just a little biased (insert sarcasm here!) and need to offer this disclosure: I invented the Armed ID arm banner! I designed it with several very important attributes in mind. First and foremost, it must be highly visible and quickly recognized. To achieve this, I used bright, reflective and contrasting materials and designed it to be placed in a most visible location. The banner is fluorescent yellow, with a 3M reflective strip, and is imprinted with a bold identifier, such as *POLICE* or *SHERIFF*. Most importantly, it is designed to be worn on the forearm of your support arm. When you are armed and in plainclothes, it is easy for uniformed law enforcement officers to see this banner no matter what angle they approach. Since law enforcement officers are trained to look at the hands, they will certainly see the banner.

In addition to being highly visible due to its materials and location of wear, I realized that no matter how effective an item is, it will be totally worthless if it is not with you when you need it. If it is sitting in your car when shots ring out while you're visiting the mall, then you simply won't use it. If it requires a special carrying case or gets in your way, then you probably won't keep it with you all the time. So I designed it to fold flat next to your wallet in your back pocket.

Finally, it needs to fit on your arm easily and quickly. If you have to adjust it while in the field, then valuable time is wasted. So I designed it to be pre-adjusted, but it will stretch over any jacket, sweater or hoodie that you may be wearing. I truly believe this is a very effective design.

Armed ID Arm Banner (armed-id.com)

You can't always be in uniform and you can't always have an identifying vest with you. Whether you get one of my Armed ID banners, an Israeli cap or the DSM sash, you need more than just a badge when responding to an active attacker while off-duty or in plainclothes. You owe it to your loved ones as well as your brothers and sisters in blue to make sure you are easily identified as a friendly.

I know, this chapter ended up being somewhat of a shameless attempt to promote a product, an infomercial of such, and I should apologize, but I won't. I truly believe that law enforcement officers need something, anything, to help easily identify themselves when not in uniform. Please take this seriously and find some way to make sure you are easily identified.

CHAPTER SIX Sources

New York State Task Force on Police-on-Police Shootings. *Reducing Inherent Danger: Report of the Task Force on Police-on-Police Shootings.* 2010. https://sites.hks.harvard.edu/criminaljustice-backup/publications/Police-on-Police_Shootings.pdf

Texas State University. Advanced Law Enforcement Rapid Response Training. *ALERRT Active Shooter Response Level I.* Version 6. 2015

www.dsmsafety.com. *Police Safety Banner Products for Crime Scene Identification*, www.dsmsafety.com/law-enforcement.html.

Cherries. "CHERRIES POCKET-FOLDING HIGH VIZ CAP." *Cherries*, www.cherriescounterterror.com/products/lowvizhighviz-critical-intervention-concealed-carry-hat.

Armed ID Arm Banners. *Armed ID*, armed-id.com/ArmBanners.aspx

PART
II

CHAPTER SEVEN

MY DISCERNED CONVICTIONS ON KILLING AND CATHOLICISM

What I wrote in the *Introduction* about myself and my convictions comes from years of discernment. It comes from my personal battle, as a clergyman, with being armed on a daily basis and potentially using deadly force that could result in the killing of another human being. This has been a back and forth battle of mine for years. After all, we are called to peace, to love each other as Christ loves us, to see Christ in our fellow man, and when you think of a clergyman, a chaplain, many images come into mind. Most likely, however, your image of a chaplain or clergyman does not involve that chaplain or clergyman being armed. As I wrote in *Chapter Five*, policies that prevent military or police chaplains from arming themselves could send an unintended and flawed message that being unarmed is a requirement to be closer to God.

I am sharing this with you because if I am going to write about your discernment on this matter as a law enforcement officer, then it will help for you to know what perspective I have. If I write without offering this background, then your response will probably be something like, "Well, you don't have to deal with all of this in the way that we do."

It reminds me of the time my uncle's pastor preached on Sunday to the congregation that they need to pray all the time throughout the day, every day, even at work. My uncle confronted the pastor after the service and said, "It's easy for you to say to pray all day long because it's your job. But for the rest of us working in the real world, well, we simply can't do that." So if I don't give you my background, you are likely to say, "Yeah, that may apply to you as a member of the clergy and as a police chaplain, but not to me as a law enforcement officer." The fact of the matter is that we are all charged with the responsibility of preserving justice and protecting life. You just happen to get paid for it.

I'll begin my story of discernment with the conflicting message that is often found in the world of Catholics. Our Church is the Church of monks and monasteries, nuns and convents. My Church offers a solid defense for the protection of life, including protests of abortion clinics as well as death row. Life is the most important gift from God, and we are called to protect it by all means. While this may ring a bell of pacifism, those who follow the teaching of the Church can't ignore the call to protect all life, including their own life and the life of their loved ones.

We Catholics, for better or worse, have a specific structure that guides us. Of course, we have the Bible, but we also have the hierarchy, specifically the bishops who oversee the handing on of the Apostolic Faith. We also have a text that contains the fundamental Christian truths held by the Catholic Church that is organized in a way that helps the faithful understand the teachings of the Church. I am referring to the *Catechism of the Catholic Church*, which is intended to be a resource or point of reference for the teachings of the Church.

We are blessed to have this sort of instruction manual on how to live as followers of Jesus. We rarely need to guess or second-guess the teaching of our Church. So although the love for and protection of life, all life, may feed the arguments of the pacifists, our Church is very clear. Pacifism is rarely an option. In fact, as we will learn shortly, it is not an option for those responsible for the lives of others.

The *Catechism of the Catholic Church* clearly states, "The legitimate defense of persons and societies is not an exception to the prohibition against the murder of the innocent that constitutes intentional killing" (CCC 2263). In other words, killing as a legitimate defense is not an exception to God's commandment not to murder. Why? Because this kind of killing is not murder, so it is not an exception, it is something altogether different. The commandment is written, "Thou shalt not kill," but the commentary *A Handbook on Exodus* explains, "This commandment uses a word that means to kill someone, but it refers to unlawful killing, not the kind of killing demanded by other laws that the Israelites understood to be Yahweh's laws. It does not refer to capital punishment, for this is prescribed in [Exodus] 21:12–17, where a different word is used. It does not refer to killing in warfare, for this is prescribed in the case of a 'holy war' (see Deut 20:10–18). It does not always imply intentional or premeditated 'murder,' for the same word is used in Deut 4:41–42 for unintentional killing" (Osborn and Hatton).

The *Catechism of the Catholic Church* goes on to reference Saint Thomas Aquinas' doctrine of double effect when it states, "The act of self-defense can have a double effect: the preservation of one's own life; and the killing of the aggressor. The one is intended, the other is not" (CCC 2263). Murder is intent to kill or maybe willful neglect that causes death. The intent in self-defense violence is to protect self and others, not to kill. This is the Catholic way of saying shoot to stop, not shoot to kill.

The *Catechism of the Catholic Church* also states, "Love toward oneself remains a fundamental principle of morality. Therefore it is legitimate to insist on respect for one's own right to life. Someone who defends his life is not guilty of murder even if he is forced to deal his aggressor a lethal blow. If a man in self-defense uses more than necessary violence, it will be unlawful: whereas if he repels force with moderation, his defense will be lawful" (CCC 2264). But what is moderation? Some may see it as just shooting the aggressor in the leg or something similar in order to stop him, or maybe using non-lethal ammunition. That is not what this means. This means that once the aggressor is stopped, then the violence on our part is to stop. As a law enforcement officer, you are trained to stop the aggressor, and then render aid as possible to save the life of the person that was trying to take yours.

It also clearly states, "Nor is it necessary for salvation that a man omit the act of moderate self-defense to avoid killing the other man, since one is bound to take more care of one's own life than of another's" (CCC 2264). And it boldly states, "Legitimate defense can be not only a right, but a grave duty for someone responsible for another's life, the common good of the family or of the state" (CCC 2265). That would be all of you, as well as me, and every person in a family with the ability to protect them. This is why, according to the *Catechism of the Catholic Church*, pacifism is not truly an option.

What I just quoted from the *Catechism of the Catholic Church* will probably have little meaning to you unless you are Catholic. But because I am Catholic, it is important that I know that it is there, what it teaches, and that I discern it as truth in my life. It was in reading this document from my Church, the institution from where my faith system is based, that I came to a solid conviction that I have every right to be armed in order to protect my life and the ones I love. And, in fact, I see it as an obligation.

Yet, even with this information about what my Church teaches, I needed to make sure that my own personal convictions, my personal relationship with God, was in line with this. I can't afford to second-guess myself if the time comes to take action. This can be deadly for me and for others. Now is the time to work through this, not at the moment that I have to draw my weapon. In other words, I have to have convictions about what I believe. And so do you.

Today I am convinced that my convictions in this matter are solid, just, and based in truth. I truly believe that if I had to kill an aggressor in order to stop him or her from taking my life or the life of another, then I would not doubt my God-given right to do so. In fact, I even believe that if I neglect to take action to stop an aggressor who is intent on killing or severely harming me or a loved one, I would be failing to follow God's will. I understand that this is not only my right but, as my Church states, a *grave duty*. I am at peace knowing that, if need be, I can draw my weapon and respond with deadly force.

CHAPTER SEVEN Sources

Catholic Church. *Catechism of the Catholic Church.* 2nd ed. Vatican: Libreria Editrice Vaticana, 2012.

Osborn, Noel D., and Howard A. Hatton. *A Handbook on Exodus.* New York: United Bible Societies, 1999.

CHAPTER EIGHT

DIFFERING VIEWS AMONG CATHOLIC CHRISTIANS

While discerning my convictions regarding killing in self-defense or defense of others, it was not only important to understand my faith and what my Church teaches on the issue, but also to understand what others in my position believe and practice regarding the matter. In doing so, I searched and read many articles regarding Catholic clergy and self-defense. More specifically, I looked for articles regarding Catholic clergy and the possession and use of firearms. I found that opinions vary widely on this topic. A great example comes from an old article that I found in the *The Washington Post*. This article, written by Bill Broadway in July of 2000, was entitled "A Higher Calling Against Guns?" It is a very fitting title not because of the clever wording, but because the author decided to end the title with a question mark.

Broadway presents two separate incidents that both involved Catholic priests being attacked while at home in their rectories. The first priest was armed with a gun; the second was not. The first, Rev. Michael R. Duesterhaus, was asleep when a man entered his home in the middle of the night. When he woke to the noise of a burglar and saw the light of a flashlight, he feared the worse and pulled out a 9mm pistol. Turning on the lights, he commanded the intruder to freeze and lie on the floor, but the man reached for his belt and charged at Fr. Duesterhaus. Firing the pistol, Fr. Duesterhaus wounded the man, who then ran down the hall. Fr. Duesterhaus chased him and fired at the intruder again. When the man turned toward the priest to charge at him again, Fr. Duesterhaus fired a third shot, which the article states was deliberately placed wide of the target. The man then ran out of the house taking a small amount of cash.

The second priest, Monsignor Thomas Wells, also confronted a burglar in the middle of the night. Msgr. Wells was not armed and was brutally killed. Incidents like these opened a debate regarding whether or not priests, who are called to be models of love and compassion, are justified in the use of violence for self-defense and defense of others.

Broadway continues to write about the ownership of firearms by clergy and states, "The idea of a priest or bishop owning a handgun shocks many Catholics." However, it also points out that some believe that had Msgr. Wells owned a firearm, he would have lived long past the young age of 58. John M. Snyder, a Catholic layman who at the time the article was written was the chief lobbyist in Washington, D.C. for the Citizens Committee for the Right to Keep and Bear Arms, stated that Wells, "most likely would be alive today if he'd had a loaded handgun and knew how to use it." This comment was strongly refuted by then Washington Auxiliary Bishop William E. Lori who believed the suggestion that priests own handguns for self-defense unworthy of the memory of Msgr. Wells.

The article goes on to quote another priest, Rev. Aaron Joseph Coty, as saying, "You don't need weapons to defend yourself. There are other ways. You can talk with the person, reason with the person, get into a fistfight." While the article states that Fr. Coty finds the idea of a priest, "or anyone, for that matter," owning handguns abhorrent, it is unknown whether Fr. Coty holds this conviction due to theological beliefs or pure ignorance of the issue as is the case with many who make such statements.

Thankfully, Broadway's article doesn't stop with the quotes of Fr. Coty. It then presents the view of another priest, Rev. Robert J. Rippy, who states, "A priest, like any other citizen, has a right to self-preservation. A person has a right to preserve their life from an unjust aggressor." Fr. Rippy stated that although a priest could possess a legally purchased handgun, it should be used as a last resort only after attempts to disarm or dissuade the aggressor have failed. Fr. Rippy points out that the intent should never be to kill but to repel the aggressor.

Broadway next points to the *Catechism of the Catholic Church* and the *Code of Canon Law* and comes to the conclusion that both leave the topic open-ended and rely on the bishop of each diocese to determine whether the diocese needs a policy on gun ownership. Most importantly, the article points out that a priest who fails to defend himself from a robber seeking cash is not considered a martyr. It quotes Fr. Duesterhaus as saying, "I would love to die for the Lord Jesus Christ and His Church, but dying due to crime is not martyrdom; it is just a tragedy. And dying when it can be avoided is just a waste of a life."

Fr. Duesterhaus later served four years as a U.S. Navy chaplain and as an officer in the Naval Reserve. He stressed the importance of training when being interviewed by Broadway for his article. Fr. Duesterhaus made it clear that training includes thinking in advance of the moral implications of using a firearm on another person and, "when conditions are such that force is necessary," knowing not only what you would do, but also how you would do it.

Snyder, the Catholic lobbyist for gun owners' rights, founded the St. Gabriel Possenti Society with the goal of promoting the "historical, philosophical and theological bases for the doctrine of legitimate self-defense." Saint Possenti, known by some as the Patron Saint of Handgunners, was a 22-year old seminarian who used his handgun marksmanship to dissuade a band of twenty thugs intent on raping and killing residents in his Italian village (Broadway).

With the differing opinions outlined in this article, the reader is basically left to discern his or her own position. The main point, however, is that there is no official documentation from the Catholic Church that forbids a priest arming himself for the purpose of self-defense, defense of others, or even recreation use. For me, the next best option is to informally poll fellow clergy members, especially Catholic deacons, priests and my bishop. Living in Texas certainly skews the opinions, but in general, I have found that those surrounding me support being armed for the purpose of self-defense and defense of others.

At ordination, Catholic deacons vow to always obey their bishop and his successors. For this reason, I contacted my bishop at the early stages of this writing to get his permission to continue the endeavor. My bishop, Most Rev. Joseph E. Strickland, encouraged me to continue writing from "our faith perspective that life is sacred and because of this deadly force may at times be necessary."

CHAPTER EIGHT Sources

Broadway, Bill. "A Higher Calling Against Guns?; Accosted Priests Different Fates Move Self-Defense Debate Beyond Bible Verses." The Washington Post article, 15 July 2000, https://www.washingtonpost.com/archive/local/2000/07/15/a-higher-calling-against-guns/793fa014-d274-4252-99ac-a5a19a4c1bcc/?utm_term=.6e0419e6b15f

CHAPTER NINE

DIFFERING VIEWS ON KILLING AMONG PROTESTANT CHRISTIANS

As I wrote in *Chapter One*, there are so many different viewpoints on killing in order to defend self or others that I can in no way cover them all. As you saw in the previous chapter, being of the same religion does not mean holding the same conviction regarding this topic. People may be of the same faith and yet come to completely different convictions. Take for example, Greg Hopkins and Preston Sprinkle. Both are Protestant Christians and both wrote books about killing in self-defense and defense of others. Hopkins served in Huntsville, Alabama as the City Prosecutor and he worked with the Huntsville Police Department training officers in use-of-force from a legal aspect. Hopkins is a Life Member of the National Rifle Association and is a certified NRA Pistol Safety and Personal Protection Instructor. He has been teaching adults the Bible since he was 18 (Hopkins 34, 298).

Sprinkle is an Evangelical Christian, has a Ph.D. in New Testament studies, and was a professor of theology at Eternity Bible College in Boise, Idaho for seven years. He is a red-meat Texas BBQ-eating American who owns several guns and grew up fishing and hunting in a Republican family. His father was a member of the Los Angeles Police Department and he himself even considered joining the LAPD (Sprinkle 248). So even though both hold strong to their

Christian faith and have similar backgrounds, they come to starkly different conclusions regarding a Christian's use of deadly force.

In Hopkins' book, *A Time To Kill*, he comes to the conclusion, "Jesus was NOT a Pacifist!" (The all-capital-letters emphasis is his, not mine.) His final paragraph on this topic states that just because Jesus rarely used force, this "does not mean that He forbids its use to us under the legally proper circumstances. Rather, through His words and example, Jesus says that use-of-force is proper to defend life and home, that warfare for proper reasons is permitted, and that we should have weapons on hand for personal defense" (Hopkins 239-40).

Sprinkle, on the other hand, presents a very different conclusion in his book, *Fight: A Christian Case for Non-Violence*. In fact, he goes as far as to say police officers who are Christian and are expected to use deadly force should not be police officers. He first attempts to establish that any violence against another human being is disobeying Jesus. Then he states, "So, if carrying out your duties as a police officer demands that you disobey Jesus, then no, a Christian should not be a police officer. The big question, of course, is whether a Christian can use violence as a police officer. No, I don't think he or she can." He follows this statement by saying that a Christian can be a police officer, but only if they are not required to be armed, such as in England and Scotland (Sprinkle 248-9).

Both of these books are interesting reads and I find it fascinating how two people can read the same Bible and develop two completely different convictions regarding the use of deadly force. I read Hopkins book first and at its conclusion had planned on presenting my material here in this book without ever telling you my personal opinion on the matter. However, when I read Sprinkle's book, I felt compelled to share my personal convictions. Why? First, I could not disagree more with Sprinkle's conclusion and, quite frankly, I find his method of justification for his conclusion to be greatly lacking. This is mainly because he infers way too much that simply is not found in the Bible or in most Christian teachings. Since I knew I was going to reference his book, I wanted to make it crystal clear where I stand so that nobody would think I was pointing them to the same conclusion. That being said, I greatly respect Sprinkle for his efforts in discerning and helping others to discern such a serious matter.

Second, when I read Sprinkle's words that a Christian should not be an armed police officer who is expected to use violence in order to stop an aggressor, I became red-faced infuriated with his conclusion. I do not believe that Hopkins, Sprinkle, I, or anybody else has any right to make such a bold statement. Who are we to know whether or not you, as a Christian, Jew, Muslim, Hindu, Buddhist, member of any faith, or even member of no faith, should be a police officer or not? That fact of the matter is that this is between you and God or your system of beliefs.

The reality is that we need to discern for ourselves even if the teaching of our faith is absolutely clear on the issue. And we must come to a conviction regarding the use of deadly force. For me, the most important sentence in either of these books comes from Hopkins. "Do not consider using defensive force unless, by study and prayer, you first reach a rock-solid conviction that self-defense is legal, ethical, moral, and approved by God" (Hopkins 183).

Whether I or anybody else agree with the convictions others hold is irrelevant. For example, I also disagree with the religious or moral arguments presented by conscientious objectors who oppose serving in the military or bearing arms. Yet, I admire the ones who have truly come to this conviction and are willing to hold their ground.

CHAPTER NINE Sources

Sprinkle, Preston M., et al. *Fight: a Christian Case for Nonviolence.* David C Cook, 2013.

Hopkins, Greg. A *Time to Kill: The Myth of Christian Pacifism.* Mindbridge Press, 2013.

CHAPTER TEN

CONSCIENTIOUS OBJECTORS AND CHRISTIAN WARRIORS

Desmond T. Doss was a conscientious objector during World War II who refused to fire a gun or engage in combat. In fact, there was a movie recently made about him, *Hacksaw Ridge*. I had no interest in watching the movie because I knew nothing about Desmond Doss and the trailer that was played over and over again on television advertising the movie had a line in it that portrayed the movie as modern liberal jargon. "While everybody else is taking life, I'm going to be saving it," the actor portraying Doss states in this movie clip. I found this line very offensive because it overlooked the fact that those serving our country by fighting in World War II were taking lives in order to save lives. It overlooked the fact that the Japanese he would be fighting were slaughtering innocent lives and, like the Nazi's, would not stop their unjust killing unless the Allied Forces stopped them from doing so. And the only way to stop those criminal nations was through the use of deadly force.

When considering writing this book, I decided to watch *Hacksaw Ridge* to gain a different perspective and was pleasantly surprised that the movie was not politicized in the way I had feared. In fact, the line played over and over in the advertisements was probably just there to get the more liberal audience to buy tickets. The full length of the line in its proper context was less offensive than the advertisement clip. He states, "I've got the energy and the passion to serve as a medic. Right in the middle with the other guys. No less danger, just, while everybody else is taking life, I'm going to be saving it" (Gibson).

Doss did indeed save lives. In the Battle of Okinawa, he saved *many* lives. The Desmond Doss Council states the number of lives saved is at least seventy-five lives. The Army put the number at around 100. Desmond Doss himself estimated closer to fifty. Regardless of the exact number, Desmond Doss was a true hero and was the first conscientious objector to be awarded the Medal of Honor. Only two other conscientious objectors, Thomas W. Bennett and Joseph G. LaPointe, Jr., both who served during the Vietnam War, have received the Medal of Honor (SSS.gov).

I immensely admire this war hero. This is not because of his decision to refuse to bear arms against the enemy, but rather because he knew who he was, he knew what he could and could not do, and he was unwavering in his belief. In other words, he knew his convictions and was not willing to change them to appease others. What good would it have done for Doss to have satisfied his superiors by taking the rifle they were forcing him to take and learn to become a good marksman in boot camp if ultimately he would not be able to pull the trigger in battle? It would have most likely resulted in tragedy and most certainly not have resulted in the saving of numerous lives.

Lt. Col. Dave Grossman, in his book *On Killing*, discusses what he calls *The Dilemma of the Discarded Weapons*. Grossman states that in the Battle of Gettysburg, nearly 24,000 of the 27,574 muskets recovered from the battlefield were recovered loaded. In fact, 12,000 were loaded twice (double rounds in the barrel) and 6,000 had anywhere from three to ten rounds loaded in the barrel. He asks why this would be and acknowledges that many of the rifles were dropped by those who had been killed before being able to fire the loaded round. How does this account for those that were loaded multiple times? Grossman comes to the conclusion that "most soldiers were not trying to kill the enemy. Most of them appeared to have not even wanted to fire in the enemy's general direction."

Grossman believes that they were just acting like they were shooting, but could not convince themselves to actually shoot at the enemy. Some, Grossman believes, even went as far as "possibly mimicking the recoil of his weapon when somebody nearby fired" (Grossman 24). Forcing someone into battle who is not willing to kill is truly of no use. They either have to be conditioned to kill, or placed in another role as was Doss. A person placing himself or herself into battle as a law enforcement officer without discerning the true possibility of killing is simple negligence.

At the end of the movie Hacksaw Ridge, there was an interview of Desmond Doss' brother, Hal Doss. What he had to say is simple, but very true. "I would say anyone is wrong to try to compromise somebody's conviction. I don't care whether it's army or what it is. When you're under conviction, that is not a joke. That's what you are" (Gibson). We should know our convictions and hold them as part of who we are. If we change our convictions for others, we are deceiving ourselves; we are setting ourselves up for failure. If we do not take the time to discern our convictions, to truly understand them, then we are setting ourselves up not only for failure, but very possibly for tragedy as well.

Like Doss, Maximilian of Theveste was a conscientious objector when he was drafted into the Roman Army in 295 A.D. Maximilian believed that he could not kill or participate in any violence since he was a Christian. Unlike Doss, however, Maximilian refused to serve the army in any capacity. This was because the Roman army required soldiers to enter into a covenant type relationship with the empire by taking an oath and wearing a leaden seal around the neck. Maximilian considered it idolatry and refused to wear it saying, "I carry the mark of Christ already." And in actuality, it would be unheard of for a Roman soldier of the army to refuse to fight as did Doss. So Maximilian refused to serve and was put on trial. During the trial, Maximilian testified, "My army is the army of God, and I cannot fight for this world. I tell you, I am a Christian." To this, the proconsul Dion pointed out, "There are Christian soldiers serving our rulers Diocletian and Maximian, Constantius and Galerius." Maximilian responded, "That is their business. I also am a Christian, and I cannot serve." Maximilian was found guilty of refusing the military oath and promptly beheaded at the age of 21 (Carson 376-7).

Maximilian knew that he could not serve in a capacity that would cause him to kill others or swear an oath to the Roman army. Whether you or I agree with him or not is irrelevant. Maximilian had to be true to himself. Had he denied his own discerned convictions, then he would have perished in spirit and, more likely, in earthly life. Maximilian of Theveste was canonized a saint and is considered by some to be the patron saint of conscientious objectors (ncronline.org). However, others hold that title for Saint Martin of Tours who is not only the patron saint of conscientious objectors but, ironically, also the patron saint of soldiers (talesoftimesforgotten.com).

Pressed into service of the Roman Army at the age of 15, Martin served well as a soldier. To the chagrin of his pagan parents, Martin became a catechumen in the Christian church in the mid 4th Century A.D. The catechumenate period leads up to baptism and formal acceptance into the Church. Prior to being baptized, Martin saw a beggar on a street in Amiens, France and cut his cloak in half in order to help the shivering man. That night Martin dreamed that Jesus was wearing the half-cloak and Jesus spoke to him saying, "Martin is still only a catechumen, but has covered me with this garment." This prompted Martin to present himself for baptism into Christianity.

Once baptized, he believed that his military service contradicted his faith. When the Emperor Julian prepared a bonus for the soldiers who would one-by-one approach to receive the funds, Martin told Caesar, "Now let me fight for God. As for your bonus, let someone who is going to join the battle receive it. I am a soldier of Christ; combat is not permitted." There ended up being no further war and Martin was discharged after much humiliation and chiding by Julian and his fellow soldiers (Ghezzi 494-5).

Saint Martin offers a good example of the need for ongoing discernment. His station in life changed and he realized that his convictions had also changed. To ignore these convictions could have proven disastrous for Martin as well as his fellow soldier. And when it comes to people who have been canonized as saints or other holy individuals throughout the history of the Church, the list is extensive as can been seen at the end of this chapter. (catholicsaints.info).

Finally, how can I write a book geared toward law enforcement without at least a minor reference to the ultimate Saint Soldier, Saint Michael the Archangel? This is the account of the great heavenly battle as found in the Book of Revelation: "Now war arose in heaven, Michael and his angels fighting against the dragon; and the dragon and his angels fought, but they were defeated and there was no longer any place for them in heaven. And the great dragon was thrown down, that ancient serpent, who is called the Devil and Satan, the deceiver of the whole world—he was thrown down to the earth, and his angels were thrown down with him. And I heard a loud voice in heaven, saying, 'Now the salvation and the power and the kingdom of our God and the authority of his Christ have come, for the accuser of our brethren has been thrown down, who accuses them day and night before our God. And they have conquered him by the blood of the Lamb and by the word of their testimony, for they loved not their lives even unto death. Rejoice then, O heaven and you that dwell therein! But woe to you, O earth and sea, for the devil has come down to you in great wrath, because he knows that his time is short!'" (Rev 12:7-12)

There is no room in Heaven for Satan, so, unfortunately, he was thrown down to earth and now *we* have to deal with him! But we are not alone. We battle him with the help of St. Michael. In fact, St. Michael is given four primary duties as outlined in Scripture; the first and primary being to fight Satan. Second is to rescue souls from the power of Satan, especially at the hour of death. The third is to be the champion of God's people and, in fact, St. Michael has been considered the patron saint of the Church and of the order of the knights since the Middle Ages. Finally, St. Michael's fourth duty is to call from earth the souls of men and bring them into judgment (newadvent.org).

If you're in law enforcement, then you've certainly heard of Saint Michael. The prayer of St. Michael is a good weapon to have in your spiritual go-bag.

St. Michael the Archangel, defend us in battle. Be our defense against the wickedness and snares of the Devil. May God rebuke him, we humbly pray, and do thou, O Prince of the heavenly hosts, by the power of God, thrust into hell Satan, and all the evil spirits, who prowl about the world seeking the ruin of souls. Amen.

Painting by Guido Reni (circa 1636)

Photographed by Ray Vann
from privately owned painting reproduction.

The following list of soldier saints is here to make the point that you can be a person of God, even a saint, while at the same time supporting the use of justified violence. There are thousands more that could be listed, but this short list makes the point.

Soldier Saints

Forty Martyred Soldiers at Rome
Forty Martyrs of Armenia
Joshua the Patriarch
King David
Martyred Soldiers of Rome
Martyred Soldiers of Rome
Martyrs of Alexandria
Martyrs of Antioch
Martyrs of Armenia
Martyrs of Cologne
Martyrs of Eleutheropolis
Martyrs of Gaza
Martyrs of Lycopolis
Martyrs of Noli
Martyrs of Philomelio
Martyrs of Rome
Martyrs of Rome
Martyrs of Rome
Martyrs of Satala
Martyrs of Sebaste
Martyrs of Sinope
Martyrs of Tavira
Martyrs of Terni
Martyrs of the Theban Legion
Martyrs of Tripoli
Mercedarian Martyrs of Damietta
Michael the Archangel
Pope Saint Leo IX
Saint Acacius of Byzantium
Saint Acestes
Saint Achilleus of Terracina
Saint Adalbald of Ostrevant
Saint Adelelmus
Saint Adjutor of Vernon
Saint Adrian of Nicomedia
Saint Aetios of Amorium
Saint Aetius
Saint Agapius of Sebaste
Saint Agatho of Alexandria
Saint Albanus of Antioch
Saint Albert of Louvain
Saint Aldegrin of Baume
Saint Alexander Akimetes
Saint Alexander Newski
Saint Alexander of Bergamo
Saint Alexander of Constantinople
Saint Alexander of Drizipara
Saint Alexander of Egypt
Saint Alexander of Pannonia
Saint Alfred the Great
Saint Amandus of Boixe
Saint Amantius the Soldier
Saint Ambrose of Ferentino
Saint Amelius of Mortara
Saint Amicus of Mortara
Saint Ammon of Alexandria
Saint Ammonius
Saint Amphilochius of Illyria
Saint Anastasius Cornicularius
Saint Anastasius of Bourges
Saint Anastasius of Camerino
Saint Anastasius of Lérida
Saint Anastasius the Persian
Saint Andreas the Soldier
Saint Andrew the Tribune
Saint Andronicus
Saint Angilbert of Centula
Saint Anno II
Saint Anrê Tran Van Trông
Saint Anselm of Nonantola
Saint Ansfrid of Utrecht

Saint Antiochus of Caesarea Philippi
Saint Antoninus of Piacenza
Saint Argeus of Tomi
Saint Arnold of Hiltensweiler
Saint Arnulf of Metz
Saint Arnulf of Soissons
Saint Arnulphus of Soissons
Saint Arsacius of Nicomedia
Saint Arsenius of Latro
Saint Artemius Megalomartyr
Saint Attilio of Trino
Saint Augustine Tchao
Saint Augustinô Phan Viet Huy
Saint Auxentius of Bithynia
Saint Auxentius of Epirus
Saint Auxentius of Mopsuetia
Saint Avitus of Périgord
Saint Azas of Isauria
Saint Bacchus
Saint Basilides of Alexandria
Saint Basilides of Rome
Saint Benedict of Aniane
Saint Benedict of Cupra
Saint Bernard of Corleone
Saint Bernardo Tolomei
Saint Besas of Alexandria
Saint Bessus
Saint Biccianus
Saint Bobo of Provence
Saint Bonosus
Saint Bruno of Ebsdorf
Saint Caedwalla of Wessex
Saint Caerealis
Saint Caerealis
Saint Caerealis of Tivoli
Saint Caius of Nicomedia
Saint Callistratus of Constantinople
Saint Calocerus of Brescia
Saint Camillus of Lellis
Saint Candidus
Saint Candidus the Theban
Saint Carbonanus of Terni
Saint Caroticus
Saint Carpophorus of Como
Saint Cartherius of Sebaste
Saint Cassius
Saint Cassius of Como
Saint Castulus
Saint Castulus of Rome
Saint Charles of Mount Argus
Saint Cheledonius of Calahorra
Saint Chiaffredo of Saluzzo
Saint Cian of Wales
Saint Claudius of Terni
Saint Claudius of Troyes
Saint Claudius the Martyr
Saint Comgall of Bangor
Saint Comgan the Monk
Saint Constantine of Scotland
Saint Cornelius the Centurion
Saint Crescentinus
Saint Cuan
Saint Cyriacus of Ziganeos
Saint Cyrinus of Cyzicus
Saint Cyrinus of Rome
Saint Cyrion
Saint Damian of Africa
Saint Dasius of Nicomedia
Saint David of Scotland
Saint Defendente the Theban
Saint Demetrius of Sermium
Saint Derfel Gadarn
Saint Domninus
Saint Đaminh Đinh Đat
Saint Edgar the Peaceful
Saint Edisto
Saint Edmund of East Anglia
Saint Edwin of Northumbria
Saint Elesbaan of Ethiopia
Saint Eleutherius of Nicomedia
Saint Emeterius of Calahorra
Saint Emilian of Citra
Saint Emmanuel Nguyen Van Trieu
Saint Enda of Arran
Saint Engelbert of Cologne
Saint Esterwine of Wearmouth
Saint Ethelbert of Kent

Saint Eucarpius of Nicomedia
Saint Eudoxius of Armenia
Saint Eudoxius of Sebaste
Saint Euflamia
Saint Eusignius
Saint Eustachius
Saint Exanthus of Como
Saint Expeditus of Melitene
Saint Exuperius
Saint Fabius of Caesarea
Saint Faustus of Milan
Saint Faustus the Soldier
Saint Felinus of Perugia
Saint Felix of Furcona
Saint Felix of Milan
Saint Ferreolus the Tribune
Saint Ferrutius
Saint Fidelis of Como
Saint Firminus of Apsaros
Saint Firmus of Apsaros
Saint Florentius of Furcona
Saint Florian of Lorch
Saint Fortunato the Theban
Saint Francis of Assisi
Saint Francis Trung Von Tran
Saint Frontiniano of Alba
Saint Gaius of Nicomedia
Saint Gallicanus
Saint Genesius of Arles
Saint Gengulphus of Burgundy
Saint George
Saint Gereon
Saint Gerlac of Valkenburg
Saint Gerland
Saint Germanus of Cadiz
Saint Gerontius
Saint Getulius of Tivoli
Saint Giovanni Calabria
Saint Giuse Lê Dang Thi
Saint Glisente of Brescia
Saint Gobert of Apremont
Saint Gordius of Cappadocia
Saint Gorgonio of Nicomedia
Saint Gorgonius of Nicomedia
Saint Gotteschalk
Saint Gratian of Perugia
Saint Guibertus of Gorze
Saint Gummarus
Saint Guthlac of Croyland
Saint Heliodorus of Altinum
Saint Heraclius the Martyr
Saint Herculanus the Soldier
Saint Hermengild
Saint Hermias of Comana
Saint Heros of Satala
Saint Hesychius of Antioch
Saint Hesychius of Durostorum
Saint Hippolytus of Rome
Saint Hyacinth the Soldier
Saint Hypatius of Tripoli
Saint Ignatius of Loyola
Saint Ingen of Alexandria
Saint Innocent of Agaunum
Saint Irenaeus the Soldier
Saint James Buzabaliao
Saint James Intercisus
Saint James of Sasseau
Saint James of Tarentaise
Saint Jerome Emiliani
Saint Joan of Arc
Saint Joannicus of Mount Olympus
Saint John of God
Saint John the Soldier
Saint Joseph Mukasa
Saint Julian of Auvergne
Saint Julius the Veteran
Saint Juventius of Antioch
Saint Kallistos of Amorium
Saint Kichi Franciscus
Saint Landericus of Soignies
Saint Laverius
Saint Leonard of Noblac
Saint Leonard of Reresby
Saint Leontius of Tripoli
Saint Leontius the Younger
Saint Leopold III
Saint Licinius of Como
Saint Longinus of Rome

Saint Longinus of Satala
Saint Longinus the Centurian
Saint Lucius of Rome
Saint Lucius the Soldier
Saint Luxorius of Sardinia
Saint Macarius of Antioch
Saint Macarius of Armenia
Saint Magnus of Cuneo
Saint Malo the Martyr
Saint Marcellinus of Tomi
Saint Marcellinus of Tomi
Saint Marcellus the Centurion
Saint Marcian of Chalcis
Saint Marcian of Venafro
Saint Marinus of Caesarea
Saint Mark of Rome
Saint Mark the Soldier
Saint Martin of Tours
Saint Matthew of Beauvais
Saint Maurice
Saint Maurus of Rome
Saint Maximianus the Soldier
Saint Maximilian of Antioch
Saint Maximinus of Antioch
Saint Megistus of Rome
Saint Meletius the Soldier
Saint Menas Kallikelados
Saint Menas the Soldier
Saint Mennone the Centurian
Saint Mercurius and Companions
Saint Mercurius of Caesarea
Saint Mercurius the Soldier
Saint Mercury of Lentini
Saint Miniato of Florence
Saint Mochua of Timahoe
Saint Modestus the Martyr
Saint Montanus of Gaeta
Saint Moseus
Saint Nabor of Milan
Saint Nabor of Rome
Saint Namphasius
Saint Narcissus of Tomi
Saint Nazarius of Rome
Saint Nearchus
Saint Nemesius of Rome
Saint Nepotian of Altino
Saint Nereus of Terracina
Saint Nicander of Venafro
Saint Nicasius of Jerusalem
Saint Nicholas of Flüe
Saint Nicon of Sicily
Saint Nicostratus of Caesarea Philippi
Saint Nuño de Santa Maria Álvares Pereira
Saint Obitius
Saint Odo of Urgell
Saint Olaf II
Saint Orentius of Satala
Saint Osmund
Saint Oswald of Northumbria
Saint Ottone Frangipane
Saint Pabo
Saint Pachomius of Tabenna
Saint Pancharius of Nicomedia
Saint Papias of Rome
Saint Paragorius of Noli
Saint Partenopeus of Noli
Saint Parteus of Noli
Saint Paul Ho Hyob
Saint Paul Ibaraki
Saint Peter Nolasco
Saint Peter of Rome
Saint Peter of Tomi
Saint Peter Orseolo
Saint Peter the Soldier
Saint Phanurius
Saint Planus of Terni
Saint Polyeucte
Saint Polyeuctus of Melitene
Saint Pons of Pradleves
Saint Ponsiano Ngondwe
Saint Poppo
Saint Possessor of Antioch
Saint Primitivus of Tivoli
Saint Primus of Cyzicus
Saint Priscus of Auxerre
Saint Proculus the Soldier

Saint Ptolomy of Alexandria
Saint Quinctus the Soldier
Saint Quirinus of Rome
Saint Rasso of Grafrath
Saint Raymond of Fitero
Saint Richard Pampuri
Saint Rogatus the Martyr
Saint Romanus Ostiarius
Saint Rudesind
Saint Sabas the Goth of Rome
Saint Sadwen of Wales
Saint Sanctius of Córdoba
Saint Sebastian
Saint Secundus of Asti
Saint Secundus of Como
Saint Secundus the Theban
Saint Sergius the Martyr
Saint Servandus of Cadiz
Saint Severinus of Como
Saint Severinus of Noli
Saint Sidonius Apollinaris
Saint Sigismund of Burgundy
Saint Socrates of Pergen
Saint Solochanus of Chalcedon
Saint Solomon III of Bretagne
Saint Starus of Antioch
Saint Stratonicus of Antioch
Saint Styriacus of Sebaste
Saint Terence of Rome
Saint Theodore of Pergen
Saint Theodore Stratelates
Saint Theodosius of Rome
Saint Theodosius the Soldier
Saint Theodulus of Tripoli
Saint Theophilis of Alexandria
Saint Theophilus of Cyprus
Saint Theophilus the Younger
Saint Thomas a Becket
Saint Tiberio of Pinerolo
Saint Tibudianus of Terni
Saint Tipasio of Tigava
Saint Tobias of Sebaste
Saint Trophimus of Nicomedia
Saint Ursicius of Nicomedia
Saint Ursus the Theban
Saint Varus of Kemet
Saint Venerando the Centurian
Saint Victor Maurus
Saint Victor of Agaunum
Saint Victor of Cologne
Saint Victor of Marseilles
Saint Victor of Xanten
Saint Victor the Martyr
Saint Victor the Theban
Saint Victricius of Rouen
Saint Vincent of Lérins
Saint Virginio
Saint Vitalis of Agaunum
Saint Vitalis of Milan
Saint Vladimir I of Kiev
Saint William of Gellone
Saint Zeno of Alexandria
Saint Zeno of Armenia
Saint Zeno of Nicomedia
Saint Zeno of Philadelphia
Saint Zoticus of Nicomedia
Saint Zoticus the Martyr
Saint Zoticus the Soldier

CHAPTER TEN Sources

Gibson, Mel, Robert Schenkkan, Andrew Knight, Andrew Garfield, Sam Worthington, Luke Bracey, Teresa Palmer, and Hugo Weaving. *Hacksaw Ridge*. 2017.

"About." Selective Service System, www.sss.gov/Alternative-Service/CO-Story-1.

Grossman, Dave. *On Killing: The Psychological Cost of Learning to Kill in War and Society*. Open Road Media; revised edition. 2014.

Carson, Thomas, and Joann Cerrito. *New Catholic Encyclopedia, Vol. 9: Mab-Mor*. Thomson/Gale in Association with the Catholic University of America, 2003.

"St. Maximilian, Pray for Us." National Catholic Reporter, 12 June 2007, www.ncronline.org/blogs/road-peace/st-maximilian-pray-us.

McDaniel, Spencer Alexander. "THE PARADOX OF SAINT MARTIN OF TOURS, PATRON SAINT OF BOTH SOLDIERS AND CONSCIENTIOUS OBJECTORS." Tales of Times Forgotten, 20 Dec. 2016, talesoftimesforgotten.com/2016/11/11/the-paradox-of-saint-martin-of-tours-patron-saint-of-both-soldiers-and-conscientious-objectors/.

Ghezzi, Bert. Voices of the Saints: a Year of Readings. Image Books, 2002.

"Saints Who Were Soldiers." *CatholicSaints.Info*, 13 Jan. 2017, catholicsaints.info/saints-who-were-soldiers/.

The Holy Bible. Revised Standard Version, Catholic Edition. Saint Benedict Press, 2009.

"St. Michael the Archangel." *CATHOLIC ENCYCLOPEDIA*: Miguel Hidalgo, www.newadvent.org/cathen/10275b.htm.

CHAPTER ELEVEN

PERISHING BY THE SWORD: AN ANSWER TO CHRISTIAN PACIFISM

One of the pacifists' favorite biblical references cited to claim that Jesus prohibited the use of violent force for any reason, including in self-defense or defense of others, comes from the 26th chapter of Matthew where Jesus tells Peter, "Put your sword back into its place; for all who take the sword will perish by the sword" (Mt 26:52). He told Peter this right after Peter struck the ear of a slave of the high priest. While this particular event at the Garden of Gethsemane is a favorite biblical reference among pacifists, it is also my favorite in making the point that Jesus was not against the use of violence in order to defend self or others. In fact, I believe it even proves that he supported justified use of violence. Here is an account of the event as recorded in the Gospel of Matthew:

> *Then Jesus went with them to a place called Gethsemane, and he said to his disciples, "Sit here, while I go yonder and pray." And taking with him Peter and the two sons of Zebedee, he began to be sorrowful and troubled. Then he said to them, "My soul is very sorrowful, even to death; remain here, and watch with me." And going a little farther he fell on his face and prayed, "My Father, if it be possible, let this cup pass from me; nevertheless, not as I will, but as thou wilt." And he came to the disciples and found them sleeping; and he said to Peter, "So,*

> *could you not watch with me one hour? Watch and pray that you may not enter into temptation; the spirit indeed is willing, but the flesh is weak." Again, for the second time, he went away and prayed, "My Father, if this cannot pass unless I drink it, thy will be done." And again he came and found them sleeping, for their eyes were heavy. So, leaving them again, he went away and prayed for the third time, saying the same words. Then he came to the disciples and said to them, "Are you still sleeping and taking your rest? Behold, the hour is at hand, and the Son of man is betrayed into the hands of sinners. Rise, let us be going; see, my betrayer is at hand."*
>
> *While he was still speaking, Judas came, one of the twelve, and with him a great crowd with swords and clubs, from the chief priests and the elders of the people. Now the betrayer had given them a sign, saying, "The one I shall kiss is the man; seize him." And he came up to Jesus at once and said, "Hail, Master!" And he kissed him. Jesus said to him, "Friend, why are you here?" Then they came up and laid hands on Jesus and seized him. And behold, one of those who were with Jesus stretched out his hand and drew his sword, and struck the slave of the high priest, and cut off his ear. Then Jesus said to him, "Put your sword back into its place; for all who take the sword will perish by the sword. Do you think that I cannot appeal to my Father, and he will at once send me more than twelve legions of angels? But how then should the scriptures be fulfilled, that it must be so?" At that hour Jesus said to the crowds, "Have you come out as against a robber, with swords and clubs to capture me? Day after day I sat in the temple teaching, and you did not seize me. But all this has taken place, that the scriptures of the prophets might be fulfilled." Then all the disciples forsook him and fled.* (Mt 26:36–56)

Pacifists often point to the part where Jesus says, "all who take the sword will perish by the sword," and in fact, they often misquote Him by saying, "Those who live by the sword die by the sword." Although the Gospels of Mark and Luke both recount the drawing of the sword and cutting off the ear of the slave, they both exclude the line about putting away the sword and perishing by the sword, which is included in the Gospel of Matthew. The Gospel of John also recounts this incident but depicts Jesus telling Peter, "Put your sword into its sheath," (Jn 18:11). John also leaves out the words about perishing when taking the sword.

Many scholars believe that the synoptic Gospels of Matthew and Luke, as well as much of John's Gospel, were built upon the foundation of the Gospel of Mark. It is interesting that three out of the four Gospels do not mention perishing by the sword. Nevertheless, the Gospel of Matthew is a principal book within the Canon of Scripture and since we Christians hold the Bible to be Divinely inspired, all words of Jesus are to be taken seriously whether in only one Gospel or in all four.

The problem here is that many Christians like to take single verses from the Bible to argue a point. This is sometimes valid, but most of the time a single verse will be unintentionally (and sometimes intentionally) used out of context. A complete, accurate understanding of a single biblical verse is usually difficult without considering the words that surround that verse as found in the rest of the chapter, book or even entire canon. In addition, a healthy dose of common sense and historical consideration is often needed to fully understand the depth of a particular verse. So let's take a closer, more complete look at this episode in the Garden of Gethsemane.

First, let's look at timing. The cutting off of the slave's ear occurred at the end of the earthly ministry of Jesus just prior to Him being apprehended, judged, scourged, and finally, crucified. In other words, the apostles and many of His disciples had been followers of Jesus for a very long time. Peter, the one who used the sword, had been with Jesus for at least three years. Peter had followed Jesus's way long enough to fully understand His basic teachings. Yes, there are many verses in Scripture where Peter does not seem to understand Jesus's teachings and Jesus even admonishes Peter on more than one occasion. This is particularly the case regarding the providential fate of Jesus that Peter simply could not, or did not want to grasp. However, they had been together long enough that if Jesus had taught that self-defense or the defense of others by the use of violence was prohibited, Peter and the others would have known this. There would be no reason for Peter or the others to ask Jesus, "Lord, shall we strike with the sword?" (Lk 22:49)

Secondly, since Peter was very close to Jesus and was with Him day and night, it would have been difficult for Peter to hide a sword, or even a large dagger, from Jesus. In fact, the Gospel of Luke clearly points out that not only Peter but several of Jesus's followers were with Him and asked Jesus, "Lord, shall *we* strike with the sword?" Although it cannot be known for sure whether or not there was more than one sword present in the Garden at that time, the use of the plural in persons could mean a plural in swords. Whatever the number, Jesus would have known that a sword was present and yet there is no indication that he ever spoke against them being armed with a sword.

In fact, it is written in the Gospel of Luke, just prior to this account in the Garden, that Jesus told his disciples, "And let him who has no sword sell his mantle and buy one." (Lk 22:36) The disciples then proudly respond, "Look Lord, here are two swords," followed by Jesus declaring, "It is enough." (Lk 22:38) So yes, there could have been more than one sword with them in the Garden of Gethsemane. Yes, Jesus most likely knew that a sword was present. And no, there is not any account of Jesus forbidding them in carrying or using a sword. The only biblical reference toward Jesus's teaching regarding the possession of such a weapon depicts Jesus commanding his followers to sell something as important as a piece of clothing in order to buy a sword.

Third, let's look closer at what Jesus did tell Peter. In the Gospel of Matthew, Jesus tells Peter to put the sword back in its *place*. John's Gospel tells him to put it into its *sheath*. Jesus does not tell Peter to sell his sword. He does not tell him to get rid of his sword. He does not tell him to destroy his sword. Rather, Jesus tells Peter to put the sword back into its place. In other words, it has a place! The use of a weapon has its proper place, but Jesus was telling Peter that this was neither the time nor the place to use it.

Let's say that an innocent man in today's world is accused of committing murder in Texas and a warrant has been issued. The man knows he is innocent and his son also knows that his father is innocent. Since this is in Texas, they both realize that the sentence for committing murder may very likely be death if found guilty. When law enforcement officers arrive to apprehend the man, would the son be justified in using violence against them to prevent the arrest of his innocent father? Of course not! The son injuring or killing innocent law enforcement officers to save his innocent father would be unjust and would be a grave evil. Why? Because the law enforcement officers were doing a justified duty. The slave in the Garden of Gethsemane was essentially serving a felony warrant against an innocent man about to be put on trial. The slave was not issuing the warrant and was not acting unjustly. He was just executing the duty in which he was charged. When Peter cut off the ear of the slave, Jesus rebuked Peter because this was not the place or time for Peter to use force.

Saint Augustine, known for his just war theory among many other things, wrote in the 5th Century A.D. about Jesus rebuking Peter for cutting the ear of the slave. He wrote, "The Lord rebuked him with something of a threat, saying, 'Put up thy sword into its sheath; for he that taketh the sword shall perish by the sword.' To take the sword is to use weapons against a man's life, without the sanction of the constituted authority. The Lord indeed had told his disciples to carry a sword; but He did not tell them to use it." (Augustinus 299)

Finally, let's look closely at the reason why Jesus said that those who take the sword will perish by the sword. Again, Matthew's Gospel is the only one that asserts this line. Yet Matthew also follows it with, "Do you think that I cannot appeal to my Father, and he will at once send me more than twelve legions of angels? But how then should the scriptures be fulfilled, that it must be so?" (Mt 26:53-54) The Gospel of John also has Jesus ending the discussion with a similar statement by asking, "Shall I not drink the cup which the Father has given me?" Jesus is saying that those who take the sword as their only strength, their only hope, whether unjustly or even justly, will perish by the sword. Their strength and hope must be in God above all, not the sword. Jesus is giving the same message of the psalmist who writes, "Thou art my King and my God, who ordainest victories for Jacob. Through thee we push down our foes;

through thy name we tread down our assailants. For not in my bow do I trust, nor can my sword save me. But thou hast saved us from our foes, and hast put to confusion those who hate us. In God we have boasted continually, and we will give thanks to thy name for ever." (Ps 44:4–8)

Jesus is giving us the bigger picture, the more important point that the will of God must be fulfilled and our salvific hope is in Him alone. This is why it is important to consider the words that surround a single verse. When put in proper context, it is easy to see that Jesus is not saying that they can't be armed; rather He is telling them to not let the sword become their god. Jesus had appealed to the Father three times just prior to making the statement regarding perishing by the sword, and then again he references the Father's will right after making this statement. The overriding point Jesus was making was that the will of the Father is what should be followed. He is warning them to not let their will supersede the will of God and to always give thanks to God, not the sword. We must trust in God completely or we will perish.

I want to be very clear about what I just wrote. This is not a sheeply statement of, "Don't be armed, just trust in God." It is simply stating that we need to put the sword, our firearms, and all material things in our lives in their proper place. God comes before all and I trust in His will. I thank Him that, in His will, He has blessed us with the tools and weapons necessary to defend His most precious gift of life.

This account in the Bible is so important for this topic that I would like to spend some time looking at an example of how pacifists abuse it in order to argue for a Christian message of nonviolence no matter the circumstances. Take, for example, John Dear, a prominent writer who has authored numerous books, has written for the *National Catholic Reporter's* blog and been featured in *The Huffington Post, The New York Times, The Washington Post,* and *USA Today* as well as others. Dear is a peace activist, a graduate of Duke University, a 2008 and 2015 Nobel Peace Prize nominee, a Catholic priest, and was a Jesuit of 32 years prior to his dismissal from the order in 2013. Dear boasts of being arrested more than 75 times while peaceably demonstrating for peace. (JohnDear.org)

Dear comes across as sincerely convicted and deeply committed to preaching a Gospel of Jesus that teaches non-violence at all costs. I admire Dear's level of conviction and self-understanding. I do not, however, admire his arguments for his cause. His treatment of the event in the Garden of Gethsemane demonstrates a level of either complete incompetence or outright dishonesty. In his book, *Put Down Your Sword*, Dear tells the story of meeting with a prominent evangelical leader who served for decades as an assistant for Billy Graham. He asked his friend, "As the soldiers approached Jesus in the Garden of Gethsemani, what were his last words? In other words, what were the last words to the church before he was killed?" Since his friend supposedly did not know the answer, Dear answered his own question with, "Put down your sword" (Dear 55).

Really? Out of 59 English translations of the Bible, none, not even one, uses that line in the account of the event. Not one! In Matthew's Gospel, 48 English translations quote Jesus as saying to put the sword in its *place*, six quote Him as simply saying to put the sword *away*, three quote Him as saying to put it where it *belongs*, and two quote Jesus as saying to put it back in the *sheath*. Likewise, John's Gospel depicts Jesus telling Peter to put the sword back in its *sheath* or *scabbard* in 42 English translations, *away* in 10, in its *place* in three, simply *back* in three, and where it *belongs* in one. Again, none quote Jesus as telling Peter or anybody else to put the sword *down* (biblegateway.com). Telling someone to put something down has a different meaning than telling someone to put something in its place. Dear even titled his book after this erroneous quote!

Dear not only misquotes Jesus in order to make an argument, he then follows it by saying that these were the last words Jesus told His church. Again, I have to ask, "Really?" As was mentioned earlier in this chapter, the Bible, in the Gospels of Matthew and John, clearly quotes Jesus speaking of the importance of fulfilling the will of God immediately following the statement on the sword. And of course, Jesus speaks several other times during His Passion as he suffered at the hands of the Romans. I find it truly difficult to believe that Dear, as an ordained priest with two master's degrees in theology, simply misunderstood what he read. To me, it appears that the Bible, like the Catholic Church, does not support his argument so he had to recreate it in a way that would prove a flawed point. Am I being too critical of Dear? Absolutely not! I have no patience with someone who is trusted with the responsibility of leading others in Truth while using blatant falsehoods in doing so.

Lastly, regarding Dear, he writes that the whole point of this event was for Jesus to teach us a lesson about non-violence. "Just at that precise moment, as Peter raises the sword to kill in order to protect Jesus, the commandment comes down: 'Put down the sword.'" Dear continues, "I think this is also the moment when the disciples finally understand Jesus and his teachings. They suddenly realize that he is deadly serious about peace, love and nonviolence. He's so committed to nonviolence that he's not even going to defend himself with violence" (Dear 65). What about all of those words Jesus spoke about fulfilling God's will? What about the deeper message of Jesus suffering for the sake of our redemption, God's salvific plan and all that?

So when this episode in the Garden of Gethsemane is tossed toward you in defense of a pacifistic stance of nonviolence, remember that Jesus is the true Lamb who was slaughtered for us all. He died so that we do not have to endure death. He knew Peter and the others were armed and in fact, Jesus promoted the ownership of swords. Jesus never told Peter or the others to destroy their swords or get rid of them, but rather He told them to put them in their proper place. He never said that to justly use a sword or other weapon in self-defense or in defense of others would cause them to perish, but rather He told them to not make godly idols out of them. Jesus is our shepherd and we are His flock. Just because we Christians are obedient sheep that allow the Good Shepherd to lead us, doesn't mean that we have to become defenseless sheep and allow the wolves of our world to devour us.

CHAPTER ELEVEN Sources

The Holy Bible. Revised Standard Version, Catholic Edition. Saint Benedict Press, 2009.

Augustinus, Aurelius, and Philip Schaff. *The Writings against the Manichaeans, and against the Donatists*. Hendrickson, 1999

"Biography." *Father John Dear*, johndear.org/a-biography-of-john-dear/.

Dear, John. *Put down Your Sword: Answering the Gospel Call to Creative Nonviolence*. William B. Eerdmans Pub. Co., 2008. Amazon Kindle locations referenced, not pages.

"BibleGateway." *Bible Gateway*, Bible Gateway Blog, www.biblegateway.com/.

CHAPTER TWELVE

VIEWS ON KILLING IN JUDAISM

It appears that followers of the teachings of Judaism are rarely divided on their stance regarding the use of deadly force for self-defense and defense of others. Rabbi Zvi Solomons, in an article written for *Jewish News*, writes that the teachings of Judaism clearly state that it is acceptable to kill in order to defend self and/or others. "In Parshat Lech Lecha, we read about Avram chasing after the captors of his nephew Lot and rescuing him. There is nothing wrong with warlike defence of our friends and families, and we have great precedent in our ancestor Avram in doing this. The Halacha goes further. When a person breaks into our home in the dark, we are allowed to kill them (Mishna Sanhedrin Chapter 8) because their intent is evil, and Halacha holds us clear of guilt if we do this."

Solomons continues his argument, "The principle of self-defence is enshrined in the saying (relating to the same passage in Exodus and from the same section of the Talmud as above): 'Im ba l'hargekha, hashkem l'hargo,' 'If someone comes to kill you, rise up and kill him (first)'". He goes on to state, "There is nothing righteous in turning the other cheek. We are not supposed to passively accept death, but rather to fight and survive."

And when it comes to the type of deadly force that is justified, Solomons has no issue with using a firearm in response to a knife attack. "The use of knives makes [an attack] a deliberate, slow and personal form of violence and Halacha unequivocally allows us to shoot a person in such a case" (JewishNews.TimesOfIsrael.com).

Likewise in *The Jerusalem Post*, Rabbi Shlomo Brody writes, "The right to self-defense is well established within Jewish law as manifested by the law of rodef (the pursuer). The sages contended that the verse 'You shall not stand idly by the blood of your neighbor' (Leviticus 19:16) not only demands saving a friend from drowning or other dangerous situations but further dictates that one stop an assailant from committing murder (Sanhedrin 73a). This right was extended to both onlookers and threatened victims alike and was also applied in cases of sexual assault" (JPost.com).

Regarding pacifism, Rabbi Michael Broyde writes in an article for *My Jewish Learning* that there is a proper place in Jewish law for pacifism. "Judaism clearly has accepted a practical form of pacifism as appropriate in the 'right' circumstances. For example, the Talmud (Ketubot 111a) recounts that in response to the persecutions of the second century (CE), the Jewish people agreed (literally: took an oath) that mandated pacifism in the process of seeking political independence or autonomy for the Jewish state. This action is explained by noting that frequently pacifism is the best response to total political defeat; only through the complete abjuring of the right to use force can survival be ensured."

Broyde believes that there simply is no Jewish tradition that states one should abstain from violence when faced with violence. He writes, "It is true that there was a tradition rejecting the violent response to antisemitism and pogrom. Yet it is clear that that tradition was based on the futility of such a response, rather than on the moral impropriety of such a response." Yet Broyde also points out that there is a specific form of pacifism found in the Jewish tradition. He writes that violence should be the minimized when possible. "In nearly all situations where Jewish law allows violence to prevent an evil from occurring, it mandates that the minimal amount of violence be used to accomplish one's goal. Thus, if one can stop a murderer from committing the crime without the use of deadly force, deadly force is prohibited (Tur, Hoshen Mishpat 425. Maimonides, Murder 1:13). If one can separate combatants without using physical force, non-violent means are certainly preferred (Shulkhan Arukh, Hoshen Mishpat 421:11)." Broyde's main point in the article is that pacifism has its proper place and so does violence: "Judaism accepted that it is best not to use violence and violence was the last resort, but when no other action would suffice, violence was morally acceptable and typically mandatory" (MyJewishLearning.com).

While not rejecting the right to use lethal force in order to stop a violent aggressor, Rabbi Jeff Goldwasser certainly would like to see a world without weapons. In fact, he writes, "The Talmud teaches that weapons are, at best, a necessary evil. All things considered equal, Jewish tradition would prefer a world in which there were fewer weapons, not more. A mishnah states to this effect: 'A person should not walk around with a sword, bow, shield, lance or spear. Such behavior requires a sin offering. Rabbi Eliezer asked, "What if they are merely ornaments?" to which the Sages say, "They are shameful."' Goldwasser states that rabbis offer a famous passage to prove that wearing weapons is a shameful act, "It is, they say, as Isaiah taught, 'They shall beat their swords into plough shares and their spears into pruning hooks; nation shall not lift up sword against nation, nor shall they learn war anymore' (Isaiah 2:4)."

I can't see how that particular verse tells us that wearing or possessing weapons is shameful, but I do agree with Goldwasser overriding point that the world it depicts would be a much better world. "We should aspire to a world without guns. A gun may stop a gun, but, by that logic, we will live in a society in which the threat of violence surrounds us everywhere. That is not what Jewish values suggest as an ideal society. Judaism rejects the nihilism of a society whose motto is, 'Every man for himself'" (ReformJudaism.org).

I am sure there are those within Jewish communities who take a pacifistic stance when it comes to the use of violence for self-defense or defense of others. However, I could find no solid article that describes such a position. There are many against guns and gun violence in the Jewish community, such as the group Rabbis Against Gun Violence which bills itself as "a national grassroots coalition of Jewish American leaders and faith activists from across the denominational spectrum mobilized to curb the current gun violence epidemic plaguing our communities" (ragvtest.weebly.com). But I believe the overwhelming view on this topic as related to

Judaism can be summed up by the words of Rabbi Reuven Mann, "Judaism is not a religion of pacifism. Nor is it one of violence. It regards peaceful relations among individuals and nations as the most ideal state" (mesora.org).

CHAPTER TWELVE Sources

Cohen, Justin, et al. "Torah for Today: What Does the Torah Say about… Self-Defence." *Jewish News*, jewishnews.timesofisrael.com/torah-for-today-what-does-the-torah-say-about-self-defence/.

"Ask the Rabbi: The Right to Self-Defense." *The Jerusalem Post | JPost.com*, 2 Dec. 2010, www.jpost.com/Jewish-World/Judaism/Ask-the-Rabbi-The-right-to-self-defense.

Broyde, Michael. "Pacifism in Jewish Law." *My Jewish Learning*, www.myjewishlearning.com/article/pacifism-in-jewish-law/.

Goldwasser, Jeffrey. "Guns and Talmud." *ReformJudaism.org*, 22 Jan. 2013, reformjudaism.org/blog/2013/01/22/guns-and-talmud.

"Who We Are." *Rabbis against Gun Violence*, ragvtest.weebly.com/who-we-are.html.

standish42. "Judaism and Pacifism." *Maimonides' 13 Foundations of Judaism*, www.mesora.org/Pacifism.html.

CHAPTER THIRTEEN

VIEWS ON KILLING IN BUDDHISM, HINDUISM, & ISLAM

So far, my focus has contained a mostly Judeo-Christian perspective. While I will in no way attempt to cover the ins and outs of other faith perspectives, it is worth mentioning some of the views on killing in some of the other major world faiths. Admittedly, my resources are lacking for learning about the views of other religions on this rather obscure topic. I am far from an expert on these. However, the limited material I did find demonstrates that the Judeo-Christian faiths are not the only ones who struggle with differing opinions on this subject.

In my searching, I found a blog entitled *Serenity in Movement*. This blog has an article, *Buddhism and Self-Defense*, which addressed the issue of killing in self-defense. The author wrote, "As a South African, who lives under a cloud of an ever-present and daily threat of physical violence and death, I cannot accept that I may not use my Martial Arts training in self-defense or the defense of others. If I allowed a child to die under the hand of a murderer and did not act to stop it, I would not be able to live with myself." He wrote this because he had been wrestling with the teaching that Buddhism demands absolute peace. "It saddens me, but I must reject this teaching of the Buddha. I cannot live in a world where I must allow myself or others to die at the hands of murderers. To do so would increase my suffering immeasurably, and to take action would be to prevent a death and would not cause me suffering" (reaver330).

From what I understand, he believes that Buddhism teaches absolute peace where no action can be taken that will cause suffering. He has come to terms with the idea that limiting or eliminating the suffering of himself or others is of more importance than limiting or eliminating the suffering of another who causes suffering. Once again, the point here in my writing is not to promote or take issue with this author's position, but rather to express my admiration that he has taken the time to discern the issue and come to a personal conviction regarding it.

Likewise, a website on Hinduism, *Kauai Hindu Monastery*, posted an article entitled, *The Hindu Ethic of Non-Violence*. The author states that to engage in violence, even self-defense, is only conducted by people of a lower consciousness. "Combat through war, righteous or not, is lower consciousness. Religious values are left aside to be picked up and continued when the war is over or in the next life or the one after that. Higher consciousness people will not fight even if their lives depend on it. They are conscientious objectors, and there have been many in every country who have been imprisoned or killed because they would not take up arms against their brother and sister humans. This is the strictest Hindu law."

In the same paragraph, the writer goes on to state, "But all 750 million Hindus are not living in a perfect state of ahimsa all of the time. Hindus, like other human beings, unfortunately do kill people. In self-defense or in order to protect his family or his village, the Hindu may have to hurt an intruder. Even then he would harbor no hatred in his heart. Hindus should never instigate an intrusion, or instigate a death, nor seek revenge nor plot retaliation for injuries received. They have their courts of justice, punishment for crimes and methods of defense against the aggressor or the intruder. Before any punishment, so to speak, all other avenues of persuasion and intelligence would be looked into, as Hindus believe that intelligence is their best weapon. In following dharma the only rigid rule is wisdom. My Sat Guru Siva Yogaswami said, 'It is a sin to kill the tiger in the jungle. But if he comes into the village, it may become your duty.' A Hindu would give warnings to the tiger, would try to capture the tiger without injury" (Monastery).

I find it difficult to follow the logic of the writer. I read and re-read the words in the paragraph and it seems that the writer is mixing up the intent of stopping an aggressor with the intent of punishing or seeking revenge. He inserts a couple of sentences regarding punishment while discussing self-defense. Using violence in self-defense has absolutely nothing to do with punishment or revenge. I must admit that my *lower consciousness* simply will not allow me to think in the higher level of this writer!

I believe this writing demonstrates a common problem with people on both sides of the argument. There is often a failure to truly think things through in a complete manner. This writer has demonstrated that he sees no difference between defending and punishing. He also believes that wisdom generates some sort of super ability to talk away a threat or outsmart an aggressor. While I am a strong proponent of tactical de-escalation, I also believe that overemphasis on such techniques can be extremely dangerous. To use the tiger example, where the tiger is threatening a village, the author states that the Hindu would give the tiger warnings or maybe try to capture the tiger without injuring it. This sounds good on the surface, but the author is not thinking to a deeper level. He may think he has a higher conscience, but I will say he has a shallow logic. I am no expert on tigers, but I doubt a verbal warning will dissuade a starving tiger. I am also not willing to risk my own safety in trying to capture a tiger intent on and capable of killing me. Even with what I see as a flawed logic, I do admire the author for addressing the subject. Hopefully, this author understands his inability to ever be a protector of society.

Islam, on the other hand, does not seem to present an issue with the use of deadly force. The difficulty is in determining where the use of force is justified and by whom. For example, there are plenty of writings that state that Islam allows the use of deadly force to defend self and others, but the aggression that justifies such force, according to some sources found, can be as small as a threat against one's honor. Other sources refer to defense of self and others, but do not make it clear if Shari'a Law permits a wife to use force in defense of herself against her husband. Without doubt, however,

Islam does permit the use of force, deadly force if necessary, in self-defense and defense of others.

In a scholarly article that ran in the February, 2013 edition of the *European Journal of International Law*, Niaz A. Shah wrote, "The Qur'an (22:39) allows the use of force in self-defence: 'Permission [to fight] is given to those against whom fighting is launched, because they have been wronged.' This was the first time, immediately after the Prophet Muhammad migrated from Mecca to Medina in 622 AD, that the Qur'an gave permission to use force in self-defence. Verse 22:39 is written in the passive tense, 'against whom fighting is launched', and therefore indicates that permission is given when Muslims are 'wronged', i.e., attacked. Verse 22:40 sheds some light on what the Qur'an means by wronging: '[they are] the ones who were expelled from their homes without any just reason, except that they say "Our Lord is Allah"'. Permission to use force is therefore predicated on 'wronging' Muslims. This position is reinforced by verse 2:190: '[f]ight in the way of Allah against those who fight you, and do not transgress. Verily, Allah does not like the transgressors.' This verse was revealed one year after the Prophet Muhammad migrated from Mecca to Medina. 'Fight in the way of Allah against those who fight you' has two meanings. First, it allows Muslims to fight those who fight them, a reflection of the permission given in verse 22:39. The phrase 'who fight you' shows that Muslims cannot be aggressors. This verse prohibits aggression but allows the use of force in self-defence as an exception. Secondly, it refers only to fighting combatants during actual combat (qital). '[A]nd do not transgress' means that the limits set by Allah must not be violated: fight those who fight you or use force in self-defence. Verses 22:39 and 2:190 are the two verses that speak of individual self-defence in the Qur'an, but verse 22:39 is a primary verse on this point."

Shah continues to report, "The Qur'an (4:75) allows the use of force for defending other Muslims who are oppressed and are unable to defend themselves: 'what has happened to you that you do not fight in the way of Allah and for the oppressed among men, women and children'. Here we find a different meaning. Whilst verse 22:39 allows the use of force in self-defence, verse 4:75 permits the use of force in the defence of those who are persecuted for believing in Islam and are unable to defend themselves. The threshold for using force in the defence of oppressed and weak Muslims is that the oppression suffered must be so severe as to compel Muslims to leave their homes, for instance, genocide or torture" (Shah).

I found it difficult to understand specific rules intertwined within many of the Islamic writings found on the topic of self-defensive force. For example, when is *Diya* (blood money) owed and when is it not? When is it permissible for a Muslim to use force against another Muslim? However, I did not find even one writing that suggests Islam forbids violence or use of deadly force.

Even though I could find no writing that suggests Islamic law forbids violence or use of force, there were plenty of Muslims asking the question on faith-based online forums. It seems safe to conclude that all people, regardless of religion, question this at one point or another. Once again, I must state that I am no expert in these religions and I will leave it to you to do your own research.

CHAPTER THIRTEEN Sources

reaver330. "Buddhism and Self-Defense." *Serenity in Movement*, 20 May 2013, serenitymovement.wordpress.com/2013/04/04/buddhism-and-self-defense/.

Monastery, Kauai's Hindu. "The Hindu Ethic of Non-Violence." *Basics of Hinduism*, www.himalayanacademy.com/readlearn/basics/ahimsa-nonviolence.

Shah, and Niaz A. "Use of Force under Islamic Law | European Journal of International Law | Oxford Academic." OUP Academic, Oxford University Press, 1 Apr. 2013, academic.oup.com/ejil/article/24/1/343/438602.

CHAPTER FOURTEEN

THE COWARD OF BROWARD COUNTY?

The title of this chapter is a question. And I will answer the question, "I don't know." However, I can say for sure that Broward County Deputy Scot Peterson has been labeled with this title and will most likely hold this title as his only public legacy. Whether the title should be shared with or even completely transferred to Sheriff Scott Israel, well, that's a separate discussion for a different writing. Nevertheless, something went horribly wrong in the law enforcement response to the active shooter incident at Marjory Stoneman Douglas High School in Parkland, Broward County, Florida on Valentine's Day 2018.

After the release of surveillance video at the scene, *Fox News* reported on March 15, 2018, that the video shows Peterson standing "safely behind a concrete wall taking no action as high school students lay dead and wounded just feet away." The report states that Sheriff Israel said the video indicated that Peterson never entered the building. "The sheriff added that Peterson instead took up a position viewing the western entrance of the building – as the video released Thursday shows. Peterson remains in the area for the next 20 minutes. Responding officers arrive at the scene, taking a total of 11 minutes to enter the building from the time shots were first reported."

Peterson responded through his attorney that he is no coward because he thought the shots were coming from the outside.

However, *Fox News* points out that audio from radio dispatches at the time "revealed the former school resource officer said gunfire was coming from 'inside,' according to the *Miami Herald*." The report quotes Peterson as radioing, "Do not approach the 12 or 1300 building, stay at least 500 feet away" (FoxNews.com).

As the story unfolds and more reports come out, it is clear that Peterson, a seasoned law enforcement officer with over 33 years of experience, simply failed to act when action was needed. It is also clear that his account of the story simply does not match with reality. But is he a coward? Is he a liar? Was he following his training? Or did he hesitate because he had not mentally and spiritually prepared for such an event?

An article that ran in *The Washington Post* ninety days after Peterson's career ended as a school resource officer depicted Peterson living a life of hiding in his house with a white sheet covering the front door so nobody could see in, an alarm system that would be activated by an outside motion detector to alert him if somebody tried to approach his front door, and using his girlfriend to run interference between him and any unwanted visitors. While he may have been able to successfully keep reporters and other agitators at bay with his white sheet and girlfriend, the demons lurking in his head are unstoppable. According to the article, Peterson began questioning his actions and blaming himself just hours after the incident and long before President Trump and the media branded him a coward.

The questions of that day haunt Peterson without ceasing. Psychologists and Psychiatrists have tried to explain it away and treat him with sleep assisting medication. But the self-doubting, second-guessing questioning is relentless. Peterson blames his failure to enter the 1200 building, where the carnage was occurring, on the fact that he only heard two or three shots and couldn't tell from where they had been shot. He scanned rooftops and bushes and although he had said the shots could have been from inside the building, he just didn't know, so he didn't enter.

One particular paragraph in *The Washington Post* article really hit home with me. "How often had [Peterson] envisioned this moment? How much time had he spent studying other mass shootings, imagining himself on scene, wondering how he would react? He had gone to annual conferences about school shootings, taken a class on confronting active shooters and led annual lockdown training for teachers. He had started his career as a school resource officer years before the 1999 shooting at Columbine High School in Colorado, back when the idea of a school shooting seemed far-fetched, but now it was a possibility he carried in his mind as he walked around campus each day" (WashingtonPost.com). So he had the training, and the potential for this type of an incident was a reality in his mind. Yet somewhere there was a disconnect. Had Peterson simply gone through the motions and physical practice of preparedness? Had Peterson approached the topic in textbook depth only? Had Peterson not prepared for the personal impact of such an incident? Had he not prepared himself to kill? Had he not prepared himself for the reality that he could be killed? Had he not prepared himself for the reality of seeing students and friends that he loved slaughtered in front of him? When Peterson replays the incident, he focuses on hearing only a few shots and believes that this was a root cause of him not entering the building. Could it be that hearing those few shots simply froze him into a reality that he simply could not accept? A reality that he simply had not truly been emotionally, mentally or spiritually prepared to address?

What about you? If you're reading this, you have most likely, like Peterson, imagined yourself in such an incident. You've thought about how you might respond. You've probably had the training, attended the conferences, read the books, and think you're prepared. But are you? Have you truly thought about it in reality? In law enforcement, the realities of having to kill and being killed in the line of duty are always with you. But like breathing, you can become so accustomed to their presence that you rarely think about them. Occasionally something will happen that will bring the thought of killing and being killed back into reality, but for the most part, you forget about them. You may even intentionally shove these realities aside. And who can blame you? After all, nobody wants to truly consider killing another human being or being killed by another human being. But you must!

As I wrote in *Chapter Two* above, you should address these

realities thoroughly, personally and frequently. By *thoroughly* I mean that it is not good enough to train and prepare physically, but you should train mentally and spiritually as well. By *personally*, I mean that your training needs to be at a personal level. And *frequently* means not just at a regular training or practice session, but perpetually.

I've wrestled with whether or not to include the Peterson account in this writing. It could be relevant, but then again, it could have nothing to do with the topic at hand and could just simply be the flaw of an individual. After watching an interview of him by Savannah Guthrie on NBC's *Today*, I truly have mixed feelings. As much as I want to believe his account of what happened and his reasoning behind it, something just doesn't ring true.

Peterson stated that he heard gunshots from outside and that is why he did not enter the building. During the interview, Peterson stated that the recent Las Vegas shooting was fresh on his mind and, at some point during the incident at his school, he thought that the shooter might have been shooting outside from a position inside the 1200 building. Guthrie pressed Peterson on this and asked why he did not go into the building if he thought there was a shooter shooting from the inside of the building. "I guess that you didn't know, but you think there's a chance that there's a shooter shooting out from Building 12, rather than stand there why not run up there and see if there is?" Peterson responded, "It just never even dawned on me those first few minutes that there was even an active shooter inside." How in hell could it not dawn on Peterson that there's an active shooter inside if he thought, by his own words 90-seconds earlier in the interview, "I believed there was a sniper. So in my mind I'm thinking to myself there's possibly maybe somebody up in there shooting out." When Guthrie pushed the issue further and asked Peterson why he didn't go inside, "Why not check it out," Peterson responded, "What I was trained, is you contain the area" (TODAY.com). At this point in my writing, I realized that although I did not believe this to be a true statement, I had not been trained in this area and could not write from an experienced perspective. In order to be able to write from first-hand experience, I took the two-day Texas State University's Advanced Law Enforcement Rapid

Response Training (ALERRT) Level I training course. This training teaches the basics of law enforcement response to active attacker incidents. Within the first few minutes of the training, I realized that Peterson could not have been trained in recent years to contain the area by standing outside, without movement.

In the classroom portion of the course, the very first presentation was regarding the 1999 shooting at Columbine High School in Littleton, Colorado. It was pointed out that, in those days, training dictated that patrol officers responding to such an incident would stage, contain the area, and call in SWAT. The deadly carnage imposed by the killers of Columbine while patrol officers waited outside for SWAT to respond was simply unacceptable. This began a pendulum swing in law enforcement response to such incidents to the point where an officer on scene, whether alone or with a team, immediately moves directly to the threat if shots are heard. The nature of the unknown, especially not knowing where the attacker is located, is always at hand. Training today dictates that movement is a must and staging, or containing a safe area, is the way of the past. I would imagine that in the last decade all training courses on the topic of an active shooter have used the case study of Columbine. ALERRT, which was named the National Standard in Active Shooter Training by the FBI in 2013, certainly uses the events of Columbine as a teaching tool (ALERRT.org). I am sure that others, such as ALICE (Alert, Lockdown, Inform, Counter, Evacuate) and the Active Shooter Threat Training Program (ASTTP), also train to similar standards and use the horrific event at Columbine as a model of what *not* to do. Yet Peterson did exactly that; stood by and waited for others to respond. This is not what is taught. If he was recently trained this way, then shame on Broward County. If he has not been trained in recent years, then shame again on Broward County and shame on Peterson!

The ALERRT course also highlighted the 2008 incident in Mumbai, India, when Islamic extremists launched a symphonic attack against the city. Ten terrorists split up into three two-man teams and one four-man team. At the Chhatrapati Shivaji Terminus train station, a two-man team open-fired on the thousands of travelers waiting for trains. There were numerous law enforcement officers inside the train station at the time, but they were ill-equipped with only British .303 bolt-action rifles from the 1950's. They responded by running from the shooter who was armed with an AK-56, the Chinese version of an automatic AK-47. Many of these officers were seen with their heads down hiding behind buildings out of fear. When interviewed, one of the officers stated, "Our brains just froze." One of our ALERRT instructors stated that this freezing was most likely due to a lack of training and practice. Ongoing training and practice take the burden off the brain as it solidifies the needed action into the subconscious mind. We know this as *muscle memory*. It could very well be that Eric Peterson simply had not received enough training and practice.

Is Eric Peterson a coward? I don't know. I have my opinions, but it's simply not for me to decide. Was Eric Peterson prepared to engage and eliminate the threat? No. Preparedness dictates that all self-imposed obstacles to action are to be removed and that action becomes the automatic reaction to a particular event.

CHAPTER FOURTEEN Sources

Lam, Katherine. "Broward Deputy Scot Peterson Seen Standing Outside during Florida School Shooting in New Video." *Fox News*, FOX News Network, 15 Mar. 2018, www.foxnews.com/us/2018/03/15/broward-deputy-scot-peterson-seen-standing-outside-during-florida-school-shooting-in-new-video.html.

Saslow, Eli. "'It Was My Job, and I Didn't Find Him': Stoneman Douglas Resource Officer Remains Haunted by Massacre." *The Washington Post*, WP Company, 4 June 2018, www.washingtonpost.com/national/it-was-my-job-and-i-didnt-find-him-stoneman-douglas-resource-officer-remains-haunted-by-massacre/2018/06/04/796f1c16-679d-11e8-9e38-24e693b38637_story.html?noredirect=on&utm_term=.32e3a2391c7b.

TodayShow. "Parkland Officer Scot Peterson: 'I Never Thought of Being Scared'." *TODAY.com*, Msnbc.com Contributor, www.today.com/video/parkland-officer-scot-peterson-i-never-thought-of-being-scared-1248443459562.

Advanced Law Enforcement Rapid Response Training: About ALERRT, alerrt.org/page/about.

CHAPTER FIFTEEN

A CONTROVERSIAL CHAPTER ON THE SANCTITY OF LIFE

This chapter is a little off topic, but I offer it as an example of the ongoing need to discern something of importance. My point here is to show how we sometimes hold convictions that have not been completely discerned and, when we dig deeper by truly discerning our positions, we learn that what we believe sometimes falls apart. As I've written throughout this book, when it comes to killing for the sake of stopping an aggressor, the time to have completed your discernment and discovered your true conviction is long before you actually need to use deadly force. In addition, we change and the teachings of our faith structure also can change over time which results in the need to re-discern our convictions.

While I may not understand all faiths and systems of beliefs, I do understand that all people have a system of beliefs of some kind. Even if they believe that everything is what it is because of chance with no creator involved, that within itself is a system of beliefs. They may not believe in a creator, they may believe that we come from nothing and are on a path to nothing, but this belief is a belief that will form their actions and opinions in life. Some believe in nothing. Some have made Mother Nature their god. Some see their inner-selves as a higher power. Regardless of what the belief system dictates, every person has a faith of some kind and it needs to be reconciled with our actions.

We also allow our system of beliefs and our faiths to be altered by the world in which we live. I wrote earlier that I am rather conservative politically speaking. I also wrote that I do not let my conservative leanings dictate my faith, but rather my faith dictates my conservative leanings. Let me give you an example. And yes, this will be a controversial example that you may or may not agree. But stay with me, because we should all be able to agree with my conclusion regarding this example.

Catholics, and in fact all Christians, are called to promote the sanctity of life in all situations. The abortion issue should be a no-brainer for any practicing Catholic. As you know, this is not always the case. Many liberal-leaning Catholics support legalized abortion. They have let the political world in which they live form their faith in action. Yes, they may say that they support life and that they are opposed to abortion in their personal lives, but they will also say that they have no right to tell others what to do. At the same time, when the State decides to issue the death penalty to a convicted killer who did decide to choose death for another human being, these same people decry the actions of the State. So which is it, life is precious or is it not?

Now, all of you right-leaning conservatives, like me, hold on before you start casting stones because this applies to us too. Which is it? Life is precious or is it not? For most of us on the right, being anti-abortion is cut and dry. And for most, so is supporting the death penalty. But why? If *all* life is precious and to be protected, what about that killer? Sure, he chose his path, we say, but when we say we are pro-life, we usually don't add an asterisk. Where is our asterisk that clarifies we are pro-life for unborn children only? For many of us, our pro-life statement should look like this:

> ***I am pro-life!****
>
> **Except in cases involving convicted criminals sentenced to the death penalty.*

For others, it should look like this:

I am pro-life!*

* *Except in cases involving convicted criminals sentenced to the death penalty or unborn children conceived by rape or unborn children who may risk the life of the mother.*

And for others, it should even look like this:

I am pro-life!*

* *Except in cases involving criminals sentenced to the death penalty or unborn children conceived by rape or unborn children who may risk the life of the mother or unborn children who will not have a quality of life due to Down Syndrome or other similar conditions.*

Finally, for others, it should look like this:

I am pro-life!*

* *Except in cases involving criminals sentenced to the death penalty or unborn children conceived by rape or unborn children who may risk the life of the mother or unborn children who will not have a quality of life due to Down Syndrome or other similar conditions or elderly individuals who have already lived a good life and whose current circumstances have diminished their quality of life.*

I will be completely open with you here and tell you that I have struggled with the issue of the sanctity of life. I am a staunch supporter of the life of the unborn. But historically, I have also been a staunch supporter of the death penalty. Do they conflict? Actually, yes, they do conflict, in most cases...for me.

The words here, *for me*, make all the difference. This writing that I offer really has nothing to do with my religion or yours. It has nothing to do with what my faith teaches. Although I should adhere to my faith, the reality is that my actions will not be dictated by my faith, but rather my level of belief in my faith or how I interpret what my faith teaches. So back to the main point, I have to discern my system of beliefs in order to understand my convictions. And then as my faith grows or changes, I need to re-discern my convictions.

For me, I had no issue in supporting the death penalty and being Catholic. I held to the teaching of the *Catechism of the Catholic Church* that teaches, "Assuming that the guilty party's identity and responsibility have been fully determined, the traditional teaching of the Church does not exclude recourse to the death penalty, if this is the only possible way of effectively defending human lives against the unjust aggressor" (CCC 2267; *see important note at the end of this chapter*). When I first read this line, it seemed clear that as long as the right person had been found truly guilty, then the Church would not be against the death penalty. However, I chose to ignore the second part of the statement that offers this solution only if this is the only way of protecting the safety of others. Just like shooting an aggressor is done in order to stop the aggressor, the death penalty is accepted only in order to protect the public or even other incarcerated people and those who guard them. Put another way, shooting to punish an aggressor is much different than shooting to stop an aggressor. If the death penalty is issued with punishment as the only goal, then the Church indeed teaches against it. The Church wants us to see our wrong ways, to confess, to do penance, and to amend our lives. The Church teaches the mercy of Jesus over everything else. So how does the death penalty for the sake of punishment fit into this teaching? It doesn't. And let's face it, and be honest, there are usually other ways in our modern world to protect society short of killing the imprisoned aggressor. We usually invoke the death penalty as a deterrent for others, as justice for the survivors of the victims, and for economic purposes. Keeping a serial killer in jail for life, for example, is very costly. So we turn to the death penalty not out of protection of society as much as we do to make ourselves feel better knowing that ultimate justice has been served.

Again, my actions and my thoughts will be dictated by my understanding of the teachings. So when I read that the death penalty is okay, I'm okay with it too. But when I read deeper into what is being said and come to deeper understandings, I begin having issues with the death penalty. If mercy is the message, and we are told to be merciful as our Heavenly Father is merciful, then how do we justify the death penalty for the sake of punishment?

When I initially discerned this, I realized that no matter my intellectual discernment on the topic, I would need to be honest with myself to come to a true conclusion of my convictions. Asking myself how I felt about the death penalty was simply inadequate. As was discussed in *Chapter Four*, I need to make it more personal. So I asked myself how I would feel if a thug in a drug-induced rage killed my first born child, my daughter Mary. Would I want the death penalty applied to that thug? The honest answer is yes. In fact, if I truly think about how I would feel, I would want to be there when the punishment was implemented and would probably beg to lower the lever or make the injection myself. That is as honest as I can possibly be. So in this case, I am a proponent the death penalty.

But what happens when I change the circumstances? What if that thug who killed an innocent child in a drug-induced rage was my daughter Mary? How would I feel then? I would beg the State to show mercy. I would tell them how she was truly a good girl, who just got tangled up with the wrong crowd, and had done something incredibly stupid. I would want her to live so that she could have time to truly repent, turn back to God and ask forgiveness. In this case, I would be an opponent of the death penalty. This is the honest truth about myself. So I realized that I am for the death penalty when I am the victim, and I am against it when it will kill the one I love. Am I a hypocrite? Yes! We all are to some degree.

In reality, however, I know that my daughter is not a drug-crazed killer. And I also realize that sanctity of life demands that all life be given the highest respect and killing should only happen in order to protect other life. So in my discernment, I have come to the conclusion that while I am against the death penalty as a form of punishment, I am not against it if the goal is to save lives. There are many gray areas here, such as whether punishing one by death will be a deterrent to others considering killing and thus save lives. Another gray area is our flawed justice system in which convicted killers are released because they have demonstrated that they have changed or at least have demonstrated that they know how to deceive the parole board into believing that they have changed. This does not promote the safety of the public and it could be used as a legitimate reason to support the death penalty. I truly believe, for example, that when a person intentionally kills a law enforcement officer, the penalty should be death. As punishment? No. But I believe that the institution of an automatic death penalty for convicted cop killers would be a deterrent that would cause criminals to think twice and thus save law enforcement lives. Is the deterrent answer a case of *the end justifying the means?* Well, yes. Then again, the means of using violence, such as shooting an aggressor, to stop the aggressor's violence can also be seen as the end justifying the means. This is a moral theological debate that will never be reconciled in our earthly lives.

Again, the concluding point in this chapter is not that we all have to agree about everything stated above, I know we can't, but that we all should take the time to discern for ourselves how we feel and what we believe when it comes to these types of topics. Blindly following our faith or our political stance serves nobody well.

I warned you that this would be a controversial chapter.

Important Note

Shortly after completing this chapter, Pope Francis changed the wording of the *Catechism of the Catholic Church* regarding the death penalty. The citation of CCC 2267 shown in the text above is now obsolete. The current version of the *Catechism*, No. 2267 reads as follows: "Recourse to the death penalty on the part of legitimate authority, following a fair trial, was long considered an appropriate response to the gravity of certain crimes and an acceptable, albeit extreme, means of safeguarding the common good. Today, however, there is an increasing awareness that the dignity of the person is not lost even after the commission of very serious crimes. In addition, a new understanding has emerged of the significance of penal sanctions imposed by the state. Lastly, more effective systems of detention have been developed, which ensure the due protection of citizens but, at the same time, do not definitively deprive the guilty of the possibility of redemption. Consequently, the Church teaches, in the light of the Gospel, that 'the death penalty is inadmissible because it is an attack on the inviolability and dignity of the person', and she works with determination for its abolition worldwide" (ncregister.com).

The deterrent argument that I offered above now clearly has no way of fitting within the teaching of this doctrine of the Church. As tempting as it is to remove or alter my writing above, I am leaving it as a true, real-life example of how we continually need to discern particular issues within our system of beliefs.

CHAPTER FIFTEEN Sources

Catholic Church. *Catechism of the Catholic Church.* 2nd ed. Vatican: Libreria Editrice Vaticana, 2012.

"Pope Francis Changes Catechism to Say Death Penalty 'Inadmissible'." *National Catholic Register*, www.ncregister.com/blog/edward-pentin/pope-francis-changes-catechism-to-declare-death-penalty-inadmissible.

CHAPTER SIXTEEN

FINAL THOUGHTS

I realize that this writing isn't perfect and that my own personal agenda did indeed influence how I presented the material here. I have discerned this topic and I do hold strong convictions regarding the right and responsibility to protect others and myself. At the same time, I have no ill feelings toward others who present an opposite opinion as long as it is presented honestly. We live in a society that perpetually attempts to spin truth to match personal agenda. I hope that I did not come across as doing so.

As a law enforcement officer, you are under daily pressures that few people experience. Whenever you can find a way, even the smallest of ways, to relieve some of that pressure can be of great benefit. I pray that as you read this writing, you found yourself a little more in touch with your thoughts, feelings and your faith. The God that I know wants you to live a joyful life and wants to use you to lead others to Him. This is not done by your words, but through your actions. Justice demands the felon be taken into custody and delivered to jail by your hands. Love demands that you do this with respect and compassion. I've seen officers plant a resisting suspect's face into the ground in order to get him to comply, then once in custody, treat him with respect and show him human dignity while booking him into jail. Most people in the faux world can't do this. You can and do because you live in the harshness of reality. I truly do believe that you are the blessed peacemakers, the children of

God.

I began this writing with a prayer and I'll end it in prayer. This concluding prayer is not my own, but belongs to my Confirmation saint, St. Francis of Assisi. St. Francis was born into a wealthy family in the 12th Century A.D. but decided to embrace a life of poverty. Although I can't say I'm attracted to the level of poverty that he demonstrated, I do admire his mercy and kindness toward others. It is something I strive to achieve. The reason I chose St. Francis to be my saint is because of his willingness to give up all for love of Jesus and the popular prayer that has been attributed to him. If you are a person of faith, I invite you to pray this Prayer of Saint Francis.

Lord, make me a channel of thy peace,
that where there is hatred, I may bring love;
that where there is wrong,
I may bring the spirit of forgiveness;
that where there is discord, I may bring harmony;
that where there is error, I may bring truth;
that where there is doubt, I may bring faith;
that where there is despair, I may bring hope;
that where there are shadows, I may bring light;
that where there is sadness, I may bring joy.
Lord, grant that I may seek to
comfort rather than to be comforted;
to understand, than to be understood;
to love, than to be loved.
For it is by self-forgetting that one finds.
It is by forgiving that one is forgiven.
It is by dying that one awakens to Eternal Life.
Amen.

ABOUT THE AUTHOR

Raymond (Ray) K. Vann, Jr., serves as a volunteer police chaplain for the Lufkin Police Department in Lufkin, Texas. He was ordained a permanent deacon in the Roman Catholic Diocese of Tyler in 2007 and serves St. Patrick and St. Andrew parishes in Lufkin, Texas. Ray also owns a consulting firm and three other small businesses.

Ray earned a Bachelor of Arts degree and Master of Arts degree, both in theology, from Saint Joseph's College in Standish, Maine.

A proud father of three daughters, Mary, Nikki, and Kiahley, Ray praises God each day for the gift of his family, and especially for Fe, his wife of 25 years.

28671117R00087

Made in the USA
Lexington, KY
18 January 2019